Perspectives on School Mathematics

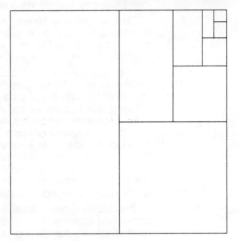

Reshaping School Mathematics
A Philosophy and Framework for Curriculum

Mathematical Sciences Education Board
National Research Council

NATIONAL ACADEMY PRESS
Washington, D.C. 1990

NATIONAL ACADEMY PRESS
2101 Constitution Avenue, NW ● Washington, DC 20418

Development, publication, and dissemination of this book were supported by grants from The Educational Foundation of America, Exxon Education Foundation, National Research Council, National Science Foundation (Directorates for Biological and Behavioral and Social Sciences; Computer and Information Science and Engineering; Engineering; Geosciences; Mathematical and Physical Sciences; and Science and Engineering Education), and The Teagle Foundation. The observations made herein do not necessarily reflect the views of the grantors.

Library of Congress Catalog Card No. 89-64176

International Standard Book Number 0-309-04187-2

Copyright © 1990 by the National Academy of Sciences

Printed in the United States of America
S085

First Printing, February 1990
Second Printing, May 1990
Third Printing, January 1991
Fourth Printing, July 1992

Preface

As momentum for change in U.S. education continues to grow, questions about the nature and goals of mathematics education take on increasing urgency. Several recent reports have opened a national dialogue on these issues. The purpose of this new report is to focus that discussion on fundamental issues that transcend particular details of current curricula or assessment results.

Two documents set the stage. *Everybody Counts: A Report to the Nation on the Future of Mathematics Education* (National Research Council, 1989) establishes the need for change in the way we teach mathematics and outlines a plan of action. *Curriculum and Evaluation Standards for School Mathematics* (National Council of Teachers of Mathematics, 1989) provides objectives for mathematics curricula and assessment that build effectively on present practice and knowledge. Although implementation of these standards will necessarily be slow for practical reasons, the expectations expressed in the *Standards* are fully attainable today. Indeed, many schools with innovative programs already implement the spirit of mathematics education expressed in the *Standards*.

In effect, the *Standards* represent goals for the first stage of a national effort to reshape mathematics education, an effort expected to last well into the next century. This *Philosophy and Framework* provides a supporting rationale for the first stage and for transition to the next stage. By suggesting a new practical philosophy of mathematics, supported by fundamental but forward-looking principles and goals, it opens a door to a whole new vision of mathematics education.

The American public expects improvement in school performance. As countless changes are tried in thousands of districts of every size and type, progress will depend on consistency of purpose. The Mathematical Sciences Education Board (MSEB) intends to keep the spotlight of reform on long-term objectives to guide the journey of all who work for beneficial change. This *Philosophy and Framework* illuminates important issues that must be clarified wherever curriculum reform is to take place. It should help advance the cause of reform by insuring a common foundation for our efforts.

On behalf of the entire Board, I want to express my appreciation to the Curriculum Framework Task Force, and especially to its chairman, Anthony Ralston, for energetic and sustained work on the early drafts of this report. The key insights into fundamental long-term goals were framed and developed by the Task Force during the early years of the MSEB. The process was guided with pragmatism and wisdom by the MSEB Curriculum Committee, chaired by Henry O. Pollak.

Special thanks are also due to Lynn A. Steen who shaped the final document by combining Board and Task Force thinking, and to Linda P. Rosen who served as staff director for the entire project.

Shirley A. Hill, Chairman

Mathematical Sciences Education Board
December 1989

MSEB CURRICULUM FRAMEWORK TASK FORCE

Anthony Ralston (Chairman), Professor of Computer Science and Mathematics, State University of New York, Buffalo

Kim Alberg, Elementary School Teacher, Franklin Smith Elementary School, Blue Springs, Missouri

Gail Burrill, Mathematics Teacher, Whitnall High School, Greenfield, Wisconsin

Robert Dilworth, Professor Emeritus of Mathematics, California Institute of Technology

James T. Fey, Professor of Curriculum & Instruction and Mathematics, University of Maryland

Shirley M. Frye, Director of Curriculum and Instruction, Scottsdale School District, Arizona

Steven J. Leinwand, Mathematics Consultant, Connecticut State Department of Education

Jack Lochhead, Director of the Scientific Reasoning Institute, University of Massachusetts

Henry O. Pollak, Assistant Vice President, Mathematical, Communications and Computer Sciences Research Laboratory, Bell Communications Research, New Jersey (retired)

Alan H. Schoenfeld, Professor of Education and Mathematics, University of California, Berkeley

MSEB CURRICULUM COMMITTEE (1988-1989)

Henry O. Pollak (Chairman), Assistant Vice President, Mathematical, Communications and Computer Sciences Research Laboratory, Bell Communications Research, New Jersey (retired)

Wade Ellis, Jr., Mathematics Instructor, West Valley College, California

Andrew M. Gleason, Hollis Professor of Mathematicks and Natural Philosophy, Harvard University

Martin D. Kruskal, Professor of Mathematics, Rutgers University

Leslie Hiles Paoletti, Chairman, Department of Mathematics and Computer Science, Choate Rosemary Hall, Connecticut

Anthony Ralston, Professor of Computer Science and Mathematics, State University of New York, Buffalo

Isadore M. Singer, Institute Professor, Department of Mathematics, Massachusetts Institute of Technology

Zalman Usiskin, Professor of Education, The University of Chicago

Calvin C. Moore, Associate Vice President, Academic Affairs, University of California, Berkeley

Jo Ann Mosier, Mathematics Teacher, Fairdale High School, Louisville, Kentucky

Leslie Hiles Paoletti, Chairman, Department of Mathematics and Computer Science, Choate Rosemary Hall, Connecticut

Lauren B. Resnick, Director, Learning Research and Development Center, University of Pittsburgh; liaison with the Commission on Behavioral and Social Sciences and Education, National Research Council

Yolanda Rodriguez, Middle School Mathematics Teacher, Martin Luther King School, Cambridge, Massachusetts

Thomas A. Romberg, Professor of Curriculum and Instruction, University of Wisconsin, Madison

Isadore M. Singer, Institute Professor, Department of Mathematics, Massachusetts Institute of Technology

Lynn Arthur Steen, Professor of Mathematics, St. Olaf College

William P. Thurston, Professor of Mathematics, Princeton University

Manya S. Ungar, Past President, The National Congress of Parents and Teachers

Zalman Usiskin, Professor of Education, The University of Chicago

John B. Walsh, Vice President/Chief Scientist, Boeing Military Airplanes

Nellie C. Weil, Past President, National School Boards Association

Guido L. Weiss, Elinor Anheuser Professor of Mathematics, Washington University; liaison with the Commission on Physical Sciences, Mathematics, and Resources, National Research Council

MSEB STAFF

OFFICE OF THE EXECUTIVE DIRECTOR

Kenneth M. Hoffman, Executive Director
Marcia P. Sward, Executive Director until August 1989
   J. Kevin Colligan, Special Assistant
   Julie A. Kraman, Administrative Associate
     Claudette C. Brown, Senior Secretary
   Kirsten A. Sampson, Executive Assistant

PROJECT AREA DIRECTORS

Beverly J. Anderson, Minority Affairs
   LaVerne Evans-MacDonald, Administrative Secretary
John R.B.-Clement, Corporate Relations
   Joan M. Rood, Administrative Secretary
Ann P. Kahn, Organizational Liaison
Robert J. Kansky, State Coalitions, Year of National Dialogue
   Linda D. Jones, Administrative Secretary
Linda P. Rosen, Educational Studies
   Jana K. Godsey, Senior Secretary

CONSULTANTS

Kathleen A. Holmay, Public Information
Harvey B. Keynes, State Coalitions
John H. Lawson, State and Local Agencies
Ray C. Shiflett, Outreach

SENIOR FELLOW

Mary Harley Kruter, Department of Energy/MSEB Senior Fellow

Foreword

The purpose of this document is to propose a framework for reform of school mathematics in the United States. One essential step in achieving reform of mathematics education is to reshape the curriculum; others include improving the education of teachers of mathematics, preparing effective descriptions of achievement in mathematics, developing better means of assessing performance of students, and preparing more effective and appropriate instructional materials. Although all of these matters are considered in this report, the central message concerns *curriculum.*

In the past century, there have been numerous attempts to change the mathematics curriculum of U.S. schools, starting with the Committee of Ten in the 1890s and including, among others, the New Mathematics of the 1960s and the National Council of Teachers of Mathematics (NCTM) *Agenda for Action of 1980.* Some of these attempts at change have had modest success; others have had little. Today, as we enter the final decade of the century, the need to achieve curriculum reform is perhaps more urgent than at any time in the past.

In particular, we emphasize in this document two fundamentally important issues discussed in *Everybody Counts* and in the NCTM *Standards:*

- Changing perspectives on the need for mathematics, the nature of mathematics, and the learning of mathematics;
- Changing roles of calculators and computers in the practice of mathematics.

These issues stand out from many others discussed in *Everybody Counts* and in the *Standards* in their compelling and inevitable impact on the organization of the mathematics curriculum. Hence they serve as touchstones for our inquiry into a philosophy and framework for school mathematics.

The complexity and inertia of the American educational system are too great for any reform to be implemented rapidly, even if it had the full and active support of all appropriate constituencies. Fortunately, the process of change is already well under way in many districts. The aim of this *Philosophy and Framework* is to give impetus to local reform and coherence to the nationwide effort. It is intended to complement *Everybody Counts* and the NCTM *Standards* by encouraging development of a mathematics curriculum that will merit the support of teachers and taxpayers, parents and students. It must be a curriculum for all students that will meet their needs and, therefore, the needs of the society in which they will live.

Contents

A Rationale for Change

The basic premise of this report is that the United States must restructure the mathematics curriculum—both what is taught and the way it is taught—if our children are to develop the mathematical knowledge (and the confidence to use that knowledge) that they will need to be personally and professionally competent in the twenty-first century. This restructuring involves more than producing new texts or retraining teachers. Replacing parts is not sufficient. What is required is a complete redesign of the content of school mathematics and the way it is taught.

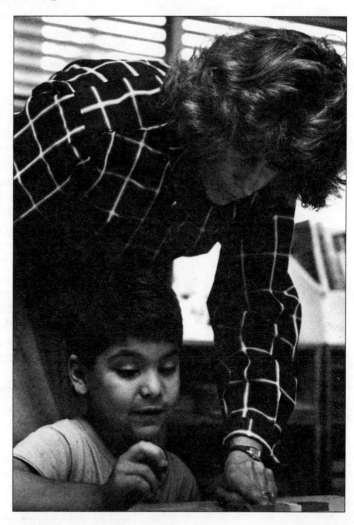

Changing Conditions

We begin our analysis by reflecting on some of the major changes affecting the context of mathematics education:

- Changes in the need for mathematics.

   As the economy adapts to information-age needs, workers in every sector—from hotel clerks to secretaries, from automobile mechanics to travel agents—must learn to interpret intelligently computer-controlled processes. Most jobs now require analytical rather than merely mechanical skills, so most students need more mathematical power in school as preparation for routine jobs. Similarly, the extensive use of graphical, financial, and statistical data in daily newspapers and in public policy discussions compels a higher standard of quantitative literacy for effective participation in a democratic society.

- Changes in mathematics and how it is used.

  In the past quarter of a century, significant changes have occurred in the nature of mathematics and the way it is used. Not only has much new mathematics been discovered, but the types and variety of problems to which mathematics is applied have grown at an unprecedented rate. Most visible, of course, has been the development of computers and the explosive growth of computer applications. Most of these applications of computers have required the development of new mathematics in areas where applications of mathematics were infeasible before the advent of computers (Howson and Kahane, 1986). Less visible, but equally important, has been the enormous wealth of ideas generated in several main branches of mathematics linked by unifying concepts of widespread applicability (e.g., Board on Mathematical Sciences (BMS), 1986). Students must study the mathematics used in such applications in order to grasp the power of mathematics to solve real problems.

- Changes in the role of technology.

  Computers and calculators have changed profoundly the world of mathematics. They have affected not only what mathematics is important, but also how mathematics is done (Rheinboldt, 1985). It is now possible to execute almost all of the mathematical techniques taught from kindergarten through the first two years of college on hand-held calculators. This fact alone—the fulfillment in our age of the dream of Pascal—must have significant effects on the mathematics curriculum (Pea, 1987a). Although most developments at the forefront of a discipline cannot generally be expected to have a major effect on the early years of education, the changes in mathematics brought about by computers and calculators are so profound as to require readjustment in the balance and approach to virtually every topic in school mathematics.

- Changes in American society.

  As mathematics has changed, so has American society. The changing demographics of the country and the changing demands of the workplace exert extraordinary burdens on mathematics education, burdens that we have not yet successfully borne (National Research Council (NRC), 1989). In the early years of the next century, when today's school children will enter the work force, most jobs will require greater mathematical skills (Johnston and Packer, 1987). At the same time, white males—the traditional base of mathematically trained workers in the United States—will represent a significantly smaller fraction of new workers (Oaxaca and Reynolds, 1988). Society's need for an approach to mathematics education that ensures achievement across the demographic spectrum is both compelling and urgent (Office of Technology Assessment, 1988).

- Changes in understanding of how students learn.

   Learning is not a process of passively absorbing information and storing it in easily retrievable fragments as a result of repeated practice and reinforcement. Instead, students approach each new task with some prior knowledge, assimilate new information, and construct their own meanings (Resnick, 1987). Furthermore, ideas are not isolated in memory but are organized and associated with the natural language that one uses and the situations one has encountered in the past. This constructive, active view of learning must be reflected in the way mathematics is taught.

- Changes in international competitiveness.

   Just as a global economy is emerging as a dominant force in American society, many recent reports have shown that U.S. students do not measure up in their mathematical accomplishments to students in other countries (e.g., Stevenson et al., 1986; McKnight et al., 1987; Stigler and Perry, 1988; Lapointe et al., 1989). Because of widely different social contexts in which education takes place, comparing the educational systems of different countries is fraught with danger. Nevertheless, the data are so compelling that they cannot be ignored. In particular, most other industrial countries have considerably different expectations about topics taught and level of performance than is common in American schools.

One implication of these reflections is the need for a new practical philosophy of mathematics education as a basis for curricular reform. Each new generation needs to step away from current schooling practices, reflect on the mathematical expectations for students and society, and restate the assumptions upon which the system for teaching and learning is based. Such reflection is especially important in a time of rapid change.

Outdated Assumptions

The mathematical content of today's school curriculum is about 500 years old. The core of this curriculum—arithmetic, geometry, and elementary algebra—differs in only superficial ways from the curriculum followed by tutors during the Renaissance. Advanced topics such as quadratic equations, logarithms, and probability are of more recent vintage, but even calculus as taught in today's schools and colleges is three centuries old.

The tremendous stability of today's curriculum depends on a guidance system controlled by two unwavering and outdated public assumptions:

- Mathematics is a fixed and unchanging body of facts and procedures; and

- To do mathematics is to calculate answers to set problems using a specific catalogue of rehearsed techniques.

These principles are the gyroscopes of today's school mathematics. Despite turbulence in schools and revolution in the workplace, mathematics education maintains its course, following a path little changed through the centuries.

To the Romans a *curriculum* was a rutted course that guided the path of two-wheeled chariots. Today's mathematics curriculum—a course of study—follows a deeply rutted path directed more by events of the past than by the changing needs of the present. Vast numbers of specific learning objectives, each with associated pedagogical strategies, serve as mileposts along the trail mapped by texts from kindergarten until twelfth grade. Problems are solved not by observing and responding to the natural landscape through which the mathematics curriculum passes, but by mastering time-tested routines conveniently placed along the path near every anticipated problem. Students who progress through this curriculum develop a kind of mathematical myopia in which the goal is to solve artificial word problems rather than realistic world problems.

Few have the stamina to survive the curriculum of mathematics—at least not the way it is now delivered. Of 4 million who begin, only 500,000 are still studying mathematics 12 years later. Most students receive little of lasting value from the final mathematics course they study—typically high school geometry or algebra II. Many of those who drop out harbor life-long feelings of guilt or distaste for school mathematics. Some of those who become disenchanted with mathematics become teachers; others help decide educational and research policy for the nation. Very few adults in the United States have had the benefit of successful completion of a mathematics curriculum.

Transitions to the Future

The price of stability is anachronism. Evidence is mounting from many sources that our present curriculum must change course if it is to serve society well in the twenty-first century. Forces for change, which are growing increasingly powerful, are beginning to redirect the mathematics curriculum in several important ways:

- The focus of school mathematics is shifting from a dualistic mission—minimal mathematics for the majority, advanced mathematics for a few—to a singular focus on a significant common core of mathematics for all students.

- The teaching of mathematics is shifting from an authoritarian model based on "transmission of knowledge" to a student-centered practice featuring "stimulation of learning."

- Public attitudes about mathematics are shifting from indifference and hostility to recognition of the important role that mathematics plays in today's society.

- The teaching of mathematics is shifting from preoccupation with inculcating routine skills to developing broad-based mathematical power.

- The teaching of mathematics is shifting from emphasis on tools for future courses to greater emphasis on topics that are relevant to students' present and future needs.

- The teaching of mathematics is shifting from primary emphasis on paper-and-pencil calculations to full use of calculators and computers.

These transitions, elaborated in *Everybody Counts* (NRC, 1989), are bringing about a substantial change in the way mathematics is taught and learned. New strategies that promise significant change are emerging in many districts and states (e.g., Denham and O'Mally, 1985; Chambers, 1986; Alligood, 1989). The ruts of the old curriculum are being eroded by the waves of change sweeping across the landscape of mathematics education.

The following chart from World Almanac *gives speeds of animals in km/hr:*

98	antelope	40	elephant	45	human
48	bear	72	elk	80	lion
48	cat	67	fox	18	pig
112	cheetah	56	jackal	56	rabbit
14	chicken	51	giraffe	24	turkey
69	coyote	62	greyhound	48	warthog
48	deer	77	horse	64	zebra

- *The human speed is listed as 45 km/hr. What do you think this means?*

- *Find the speed of the winner of the most recent Olympic 1500 meter run. How does this compare with the speed listed for the human in the chart? What explanation can you give for this?*

- *What is the typical speed for animals? How did you find this speed?*

- *How do the speeds differ? Are there any animals whose speeds are similar? Do these animals have anything in common? Are there any animals whose speeds are much different than the rest?*

- *Separate the animals into groups according to the kind of food they eat and compare the speeds for each group. What conclusions can you make?*

- *Write a paragraph describing the results of your analysis.*

Data Analysis

A Practical Philosophy

Foundations for an improved mathematics curriculum must rest on analysis of the nature of mathematics and the goals of mathematics education. Even the most superficial observation shows unequivocally that the nature of mathematics is changing, that the goals of mathematics education are expanding, and that schools are in the midst of major transitions.

Expanding Goals

We teach mathematics to serve several very different goals that reflect the diverse roles that mathematics plays in society:

- **A Practical Goal:** To help individuals solve problems of everyday life.
- **A Civic Goal:** To enable citizens to participate intelligently in civic affairs.
- **A Professional Goal:** To prepare students for jobs, vocations, or professions.
- **A Cultural Goal:** To impart a major element of human culture.

The mathematical knowledge needed to achieve these goals has changed dramatically in the twentieth century and is changing more rapidly now than ever before.

Perhaps most obvious is the change needed for everyday life. Whereas daily activities once required a considerable amount of paper-and-pencil calculation, virtually all routine household arithmetic is now done either mentally or with an inexpensive hand-held calculator. It is not just that the kinds of solutions we have at our disposal have changed, but so too have the problems. Today to be mathematically literate one must be able to interpret both quantitative and spatial information in a variety of numerical, symbolic, and graphical contexts. These changes provide an unprecedented opportunity to redirect much of current elementary school mathematics to more fruitful and important areas—especially to the new world of sophisticated electronic computation. As calculators and computers diminish the role of routine computation, school mathematics can focus instead on the conceptual insights and analytic skills that have always been at the heart of mathematics.

The changes in mathematics needed for intelligent citizenship have been no less significant. Most obvious, perhaps, is the need to understand data presented in a variety of different formats: percentages, graphs, charts, tables, and statistical analyses are commonly used to influence societal decisions. Largely because data are now so widely available, daily newspapers employ a considerable variety of quantitative images in ordinary reporting of news events. Citizens who cannot properly interpret quantitative data are, in this day and age, functionally illiterate.

It is, however, the professional and vocational needs for mathematics that have changed most rapidly. Mathematics is essential to more disciplines than ever before. The explosive growth of technology in the twentieth century has amplified the role of mathematics. By increasing the number and variety of problems that can be solved, calculators and computers have significantly increased the need for mathematical knowledge and changed the kind of knowledge that is needed. Computers have moved many vocations (e.g., farming) to become more quantitative and thus more productive. The result is that people in an expanding number of vocations and professions need to know enough mathematics to be able to recognize when mathematics may be helpful to them.

Because of society's preoccupation with the practical and professional roles of mathematics, schools rarely emphasize cultural or historical aspects of mathematics. Like all subjects, mathematics is dehumanized when divorced from its cultural contributions and its history. To the extent that these subjects are discussed at all, students are likely to get the impression that mathematics is static and old-fashioned. While it is commonplace for school children to become familiar with modern concepts in the sciences such as DNA and atomic energy,

rarely are children introduced to any mathematics (such as statistics or topology) discovered less than a century ago. Children never learn that mathematics is a dynamic, growing discipline, and only rarely do they see the beauty and fascination of mathematics. The mathematics curriculum can no longer ignore the twentieth century.

Fundamental Questions

To realize a new vision of school mathematics will require public acceptance of a realistic philosophy of mathematics that reflects both mathematical practice and pedagogical experience. One cannot properly constitute a framework for a mathematics curriculum unless one first addresses two fundamental questions:

- What is mathematics?
- What does it mean to know mathematics?

Although few mathematicians or teachers spend much time thinking about these philosophical questions, the unstated answers that are embedded in public and professional opinion are the invisible hands that control mathematics education. No change in education can be effective until the hidden influences of these deep issues are redirected toward objectives more in tune with today's world.

Yet even as forces for change are providing new directions for mathematics education, the public instinct for restoring traditional stability remains strong. Unless the guidance system for mathematics education is permanently reset to new and more appropriate goals, it will surely steer the curriculum back to its old path once present pressure for change abates.

Answers to these fundamental questions would help clarify for both educators and the public what mathematics is really about—what it studies, how it operates, what it is good for (Romberg, 1988). Appropriate answers would provide a convincing platform on which to erect a new mathematics curriculum of the twenty-first century in which children would be introduced not only to the traditional themes of number and space, but also to many newer themes such as logic, chance, computation, and statistics. From these answers would flow a pragmatic philosophy of mathematics that could help explain the creative tension that binds the two fundamental poles of mathematical reality:

- **Theory:** That in mathematics, reasoning is the test of truth.

- **Applications:** That mathematical models are both apt and useful.

One might think that the many definitions of mathematics provided by scholars in centuries past would suffice for this task. But in the past few years, as computers have begun to unfold new potentials of mathematical systems, we have been able to see mathematics in a significantly broadened context. As the *Apollo* missions for the first time enabled people to see and describe the back side of the moon, so computers have now enabled us to grasp a much richer landscape of the mathematical sciences. It is now time to reshape mathematics education to reflect both the significant role of computers in the practice of mathematics and the transformed role played by mathematics in modern society.

Describing Mathematics

We begin with a simple approximation: *mathematics is a science.* Observations, experiment, discovery, and conjecture are as much part of the practice of mathematics as of any natural science. Trial and error, hypothesis and investigation, and measurement and classification are part of the mathematician's craft and should be taught in school. Laboratory work and fieldwork are not only appropriate but necessary to a full understanding of what mathematics is and how it is used. Calculators and computers are necessary tools in this mathematics lab, but so too are sources of real data (scientific experiments, demographic data, opinion polls), objects to observe and measure (dice, blocks, balls), and tools for construction (rulers, string, protractors, clay, graph paper).

As biology is a science of living organisms and physics is a science of matter and energy, so *mathematics is a science of patterns*. This description goes back at least to Descartes in a slightly different form (he called mathematics the "science of order"), and has been refined by physicist Steven Weinberg who used it to explain the uncanny ability of mathematics to anticipate nature (Steen, 1988). A similar view of mathematics as the science of "patterns and relationships" forms the basis for the expression of matnematics in *Science for All Americans* (American Association for the Advancement of Science (AAAS), 1989). By classifying, explaining, and describing patterns in all their manifestations—number, data, shape, arrangements, even patterns themselves—mathematics ensures that any pattern encountered by scientists will be explained somewhere as part of the practice of mathematics.

Patterns are evident in every aspect of mathematics. Young children learn how arithmetic depends on the regularity of numbers; they can see order in the multiplication table and wonder about disorder in the pattern of primes. The geometry of polyhedra exhibits a regularity that recurs throughout nature and in architecture. Even statistics, a subject which studies disorder, depends on exhibited patterns as a yardstick for assessing uncertainty.

As a science of patterns, mathematics is a mode of inquiry that reveals fundamental truth about the order of our world. But mathematics is also a form of communication that complements natural language as a tool for describing the world in which we live. So mathematics is not only a science, but also *mathematics is a language*. It is, as science has revealed, the language in which nature speaks. But it is also an apt language for business and commerce.

From its beginnings in ancient cultures, the language of mathematics has been widely used in commerce: measurement and counting—geometry and arithmetic—enabled trade and regularized financial transactions. In recent centuries, mathematics (first calculus, then statistics) provided the intellectual and inferential framework for the growth of science. The mathematical sciences (including statistics) are now the foundation disciplines of natural, social, and behavioral sciences. Moreover, with the support of computers and worldwide digital communication, business and industry depend increasingly not only on traditional but also on modern mathematical methods of analysis.

Mathematics can serve as the language of business and science precisely because *mathematics is a language that describes patterns.* In its symbols and syntax, its vocabulary and idioms, the language of mathematics is a universal means of communication about relationships and patterns. It is a language everybody must learn to use.

Knowing Mathematics

If mathematics is a science and language of patterns, then to know mathematics is to investigate and express relationships among patterns: to be able to discern patterns in complex and obscure contexts; to understand and transform relations among patterns; to classify, encode, and describe patterns; to read and write in the language of patterns; and to employ knowledge of patterns for various practical purposes. To grasp the diversity of patterns—indeed, to begin to see patterns among patterns—it is necessary that the mathematics curriculum introduce and develop mathematical patterns of many different types. As the patterns studied by mathematics are not limited to the rules of arithmetic, so the patterns studied in school mathematics must break the bonds of this artificial constraint.

A person engaged in mathematics gathers, discovers, creates, or expresses facts and ideas about patterns. Mathematics is a creative, active process very different from passive mastery of concepts and procedures. Facts, formulas, and information have value only to the extent to which they support effective mathematical activity. Although some fundamental concepts and procedures must be known by all students, instruction should persistently emphasize that to know mathematics is to engage in a quest to understand and communicate, not merely to calculate. By unfolding the fundamental principles of pattern, mathematics makes the mind an effective tool for dealing with the world. From these views can flow an effective and dynamic school curriculum for the next century.

Practical Effects

The practical test of a philosophy is the effect it should have on practice—in this case, on the teaching of mathematics.

A Philosophy and Framework

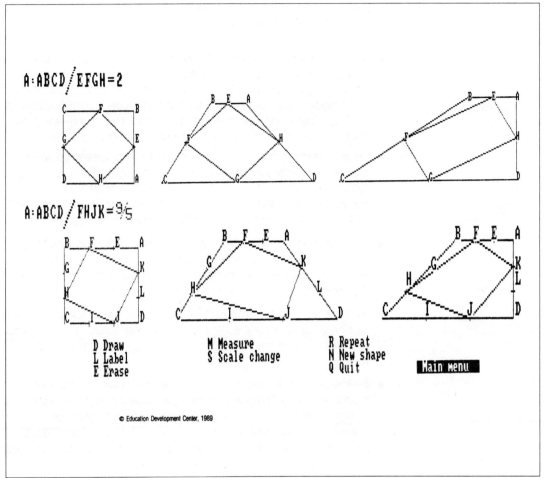

A:ABCD/EFGH=2

A:ABCD/FHJK=⁹⁄₅

D Draw
L Label
E Erase

M Measure
S Scale change

R Repeat
N New shape
Q Quit

Main menu

© Education Development Center, 1989

The Geometric Supposer is a set of software learning environments deliberately designed to change school plane geometry from a closely guided museum tour (where the guide points out certain artifacts to be "proven") to an active process of building and exploring conjectures. For example, a student who constructs the three medians of a triangle and notices that they all intersect in a point might wonder if this is a fluke, or whether it might hold for other triangles. By using a repeat feature, the student can quickly execute the same construction on a series of triangles, either generated at random by the computer or produced by the student in a way designed to stress the conjecture in some particular way (e.g., on a long, thin obtuse triangle).

In the six figures above, a student uses the Supposer to generalize a basic construction where corresponding points of adjacent sides of a square are joined and the ratio of the area of the square and the interior figure are calculated. From left to right, the construction and calculation are repeated on different quadrilaterals. In the top row, the sides of each figure are divided into two equal parts; in the bottom row, the sides of each figure are divided into three equal parts.

What conjectures emerge? How can these conjectures be justified?

The Geometric Supposer

Many important ideas follow from the view of mathematics as a science and language of patterns.

- By expressing a broad view of the mathematical sciences, this proposed philosophy encompasses all traditional topics covered by school mathematics. Arithmetic and geometry, algebra and calculus are richly endowed with patterns of number, shape, and measure—patterns that will support much of the traditional curriculum.

- By suggesting that mathematics encompasses all kinds of patterns wherever they arise, this perspective compels a broader vision of school mathematics that includes, for example, mathematical structures in probability and statistics, in discrete mathematics and optimization.

- By stressing that mathematics is a science, this philosophy supports a style of instruction that rewards exploration, encourages experiments, and respects conjectural approaches to solving problems.

- By recognizing that mathematics is an apt language of business and science, this view underscores the universal importance of mathematics as a subject that all students must learn to use.

- By invoking the metaphor of science in which experiment complements theory, the perspective of mathematics as a science of patterns helps bridge the gap between "pure" and "applied" mathematics. The patterns studied by mathematicians are, for all practical purposes, as real as the atomic particles studied by physicists.

- By emphasizing that mathematics is a process rather than a set of facts, this perspective makes clear that students need to experience genuine problems—those whose solutions have yet to be developed by the students (or even perhaps by their teachers). Problem situations should be complex enough to offer challenge, but not so complex as to be insoluble. Learning should be guided by the search to answer questions—first at an intuitive, empirical level; then by generalizing; and later by justifying (proving).

- By making clear that mathematics is the study of patterns rather than merely a craft for calculation (or an art with no evident purpose), this pragmatic view highlights the philosophical basis for using calculators in school mathematics: as microscopes are to biology and telescopes to astronomy, calculators and computers have become essential tools for the study of patterns.

- By recognizing that practical knowledge emerges from experience with problems, this view helps explain how experience with problems can help develop students' ability to compute. This recognition contrasts sharply with the prevailing expectation in schools that skill in computation should precede encounter with word problems. Present strategies for teaching need to be reversed: students who recognize the need to apply particular concepts have a stronger conceptual basis for reconstructing their knowledge at a later time.

By stressing mathematics as a language in which students express ideas, we enable students to develop a framework that can be drawn upon in the future, when rules may have been forgotten but the structure of mathematical language remains embedded in memory as a foundation for reconstruction. Learning the language of mathematics requires immersion in situations that are sufficiently simple to be manageable, but sufficiently complex to offer diversity: individual, small-group, or large-group instruction; a variety of mathematical domains; and open and flexible methods.

By affirming the importance of mathematics as a language and science of patterns we reset the gyroscopes that guide school mathematics. Instead of being viewed as an immutable collection of absolute truths, mathematics will be seen as it is—as an evolving, pragmatic discipline that seeks to understand the behavior of patterns in science, in society, and in everyday life.

Philosophical Perspectives

Changing the public philosophy of school mathematics is an essential step in effecting reform of mathematics education. An effective practical philosophy of mathematics can be based on two considerations:

- That mathematics is a science and language of patterns;

- That to know mathematics is to investigate and express relationships among patterns.

Nothing in this approach implies that these are unique or necessary considerations. They are, however, sufficient to meet certain important criteria that any effective philosophy of mathematics education must satisfy:

- They encompass new as well as traditional topics;

- They provide a substantive rationale for using calculators and computers in school mathematics;

- They encourage experience with genuine problems;

- They stimulate exploration, use of real data, and apprenticeship learning;

- They help bridge the gap between pure and applied mathematics;

- They emphasize active modes of learning;

- They are understandable to a broad segment of the public.

The framework for mathematics education that follows from this practical philosophy provides an environment to support present efforts at curricular reform. Other philosophies can also provide similar support, and surely many others will emerge in the process of national curricular change. The counterpoint between a philosophy and a framework of mathematics education will continue as long as the process of change remains vigorous.

Redesign from a Technological Perspective

Of the many forces at work that are changing the way mathematics is learned, the impact of technology is both most urgent and most controversial. In less than two decades society has moved from primitive electronic calculators to desk-top workstations that are as powerful as the largest computers of only a few years ago. The unprecedented magnitude and speed of change in technology has created a considerable degree of professional confusion and public alarm about mathematics education.

Mathematicians and parents are divided on the wisdom of early and widespread use of calculators before children have mastered arithmetic by traditional means. Calculators are seen as doing to arithmetic what many believe television has done to reading. Concern about further deterioration in basic skills fuels a general fear of change that has produced a sustained public debate about the wisdom of calculator use. Many who view mathematics as an ideal instrument to filter students into professional and educational tracks believe that calculators make this filtering less effective—by enabling too many students to score well despite weakness in traditional skills. The image of a calculator as an inappropriate intellectual crutch is so deeply ingrained in many adult's minds—especially among mathematicians and scientists—that most college entrance exams do not permit calculator use.

Advocates of early and unrestricted use of calculators—including virtually all mathematics educators—argue on the basis of student motivation, classroom realism, and needs of the workplace. Calculators are seen as an effective tool to transform the typical arithmetic lesson from worksheet drudgery into motivated exploration. Appropriate use of calculators can enhance opportunity for children to learn higher-order thinking skills without first mastering standard computational algorithms. Indeed, early informal experience with multiple approaches to arithmetic problems—including calculators, fingers, and other devices—provides a secure base for subsequent study of standard techniques. Calculators enable curricula to move beyond emphasis on mechanics to experience with ideas.

In contrast to calculators, use of computers in the schools is rather widely supported by the general public. However, among mathematicians and classroom teachers, their use is just as controversial as calculators—and for essentially the same reasons. Many mathematicians and teachers fear that time spent learning to use computer programs—whether it be programming languages such as Logo or Basic or packages such as Mathematica—is time subtracted from what they believe to be the central lessons of mathematics: solving problems with paper, pencil, and pure thought. Electronic aids like computers should be used by professionals to implement quickly and accurately what they have already learned, not used in education as an alternative to traditional techniques for developing skill and understanding.

Despite the controversy, most mathematics educators who have studied the issues and the evidence have concluded that the potential benefit to mathematics education is enormous, well worth the extra effort and increased risk associated with venturing into uncharted territory (Wilf, 1982; Fey, 1984; Hansen, 1984; Smith et al., 1988). Increased use of technology in mathematics education is inevitable, but wise use is not automatic. Technology has more to offer education than just high-tech flash cards. Effective use of calculators and computers requires objectives for mathematics education that are aligned with the mathematical needs of the information age.

New Opportunities

From four-function calculators to desk-top workstations, computer technology is poised to make an extraordinary impact on the content and presentation of mathematics education. Computing devices will:

- Decrease the value of many manual skills traditionally taught in the school mathematics curriculum;

- Increase the importance of many areas of mathematics that now are rarely taught;
- Focus attention as much on problem formulation as on problem solving;
- Make possible tools for teaching and learning of a sophistication still largely undreamed of by most mathematics educators.

More than any other empowerment of technology, computer graphics will, in particular, totally transform the way mathematics is used. Because the United States still leads the world in most aspects of computer technology, we have a unique opportunity to grasp the potential of this technology and use it to make dramatic improvements in mathematics education.

> Use a calculator to find three different numbers whose product is 7429. How many different answers can you find? Write a paragraph explaining what you did, why you did it, and how well it worked.

Exploring Numbers

A growing volume of research supports appropriate use of calculators in any grade. It is now clear that an understanding of arithmetic can be developed with a curriculum that uses estimation, mental arithmetic, and calculators, with reduced instruction in manual calculation. Indeed, mental arithmetic may replace written methods as the basic skill of our computer age.

Since few arithmetic calculations are done most efficiently using paper and pencil, the level of arithmetic skill that is the current goal in most elementary school classrooms is far in excess of what is needed for tomorrow's society. Indeed, there is some evidence that overemphasis on manual skills hinders the child's learning of when and how to use them. Too often, skill rather than meaning becomes the message.

Thus, any reform of school mathematics must entail a major reduction in the time spent on teaching traditional arithmetic skills. Technological developments suggest strongly that even those aspects of the secondary school curriculum that are oriented mainly to development of algebraic skills such as polynomial arithmetic no longer serve a compelling purpose. In a computer age, facility in these skills is not an absolute prerequisite either to the use of mathematics or to further study in mathematically based fields.

New Priorities

Reducing priority on development of routine skills will allow a variety of desirable consequences. There will be more time to develop understanding of processes and reasoning that lie at the heart of mathematical problem solving (Conference Board of the Mathematical Sciences (CBMS), 1983). Indeed, enabling students to solve a variety of problems is one of the main purposes of school mathematics education.

By reducing emphasis on manual skills, it will be easier to develop a curriculum that will allow *all* students some level of mathematical accomplishment while retaining the interest and enthusiasm of the more able students. The current emphasis on manual arithmetic skills, which any observant student knows are seldom used outside school, contributes to distaste for mathematics in many able students. For slower students who fail to achieve quick mastery of arithmetic skills, there is no path to future success in mathematics. Less stress on skills will make possible an elementary school mathematics curriculum in which lack of success in one area will not necessarily preclude success in another.

In such a curriculum, it will be possible to emphasize approximation and estimation, topics that play essential roles in many areas of mathematics (Schoen, 1986). Is it more important for a student to be able to multiply 2507 x 4131 precisely or to be able to say that the result is about 10 million? Often, the approximate answer is not only sufficient, but it also provides more insight than the exact answer. Moreover, the approximate answer provides a quick check on the result of any exact procedure, whether by a hand moving a pencil or by fingers pushing buttons on a calculator.

A broader curriculum stressing a variety of mathematical strategies will make it possible to teach material to students in each grade that will be useful to them no matter when they end their mathematics education. At the same time, students preparing for further study of mathematics will be stimulated by early glimpses—via the power of the computer—of what lies ahead.

Finally, computers and calculators have changed not only what mathematics is important, but also how mathematics should be taught (Zorn, 1987):

- *Computers and calculators change what is feasible and what is important.* They make the difficult easy and the infeasible possible. For example, computers can display and manipulate mathematical objects such as complicated three-dimensional forms that cannot reasonably be studied without computers. As a consequence, students can solve realistic problems that are relevant to their everyday experiences and that have the potential of stimulating continuing interest in mathematics.

- *Computers free the teacher for those tasks that only a teacher can do.* For example, teacher and students can together explore conjectures. Computers provide a dynamic and graphic medium that offers many effective ways to present mathematical ideas.

- *Technology makes mathematics realistic.* Before the advent of calculators and computers, even the most able students could not perform calculations required for most realistic problems. Nor, for that matter, could teachers do such calculations for students without spending far too much time on the computations themselves. Now, computation itself is no longer a barrier. If the problem can be grasped by the students, then it can be solved. Real data from real experiments can be analyzed. Equations that represent significant physical situations can be solved. Many sophisticated concepts can be made more intelligible with computers than through any other means.

The Year 2000

The eventual use of technology in the teaching and learning of mathematics can be seen, at best, only dimly today. Few classrooms today are equipped to make the use of computers convenient and inviting for teachers. Software, even when of high quality, is often relevant only to narrow curricular objectives. Too often it is neither teacher-friendly nor student-friendly. Rarely is it coordinated with textbooks or curriculum. Despite these current problems, which are legacies of old technology, workstations of the 1990s will offer powerful, flexible environments that will make possible a much improved symbiosis between teacher and technology.

Developments in computer technology, both hardware and software, are notoriously hard to predict. Still, enough is known now to be able to make some reasonable predictions about what is desirable and feasible for computers in schools in the year 2000:

- All students should have available hand-held calculators with a functionality appropriate to their grade level. Calculators suitable for secondary school will by then have symbolic and graphics capability sufficient for all high-school level mathematics.

- All mathematics classrooms should have permanently installed contemporary computers with display units conveniently visible by all students. New schools may be equipped with desks that include built-in computers.

- There should be sufficient computer facilities available for laboratory and out-of-classroom needs of all students. In

particular, portable computers should by then be available for students to borrow overnight as they would a book from the library.

Facilities like these are beyond the budgets of most school districts today. However, by 2000 their relative cost should be much less than it is today. Districts need to plan now to ensure calculator and computer facilities adequate for all classes and all students. School boards and administrators must plan school budgets to ensure full access to the tools of learning, especially for districts with limited resources. This is an area in which government, business, and industry can effectively enhance education by cooperating on a plan to ensure full technological support in every classroom in America. Curricular blueprints developed today must be based on the technological reality of tomorrow's schools.

Research Findings

Of all the influences that shape mathematics education, technology stands out as the one with greatest potential for revolutionary impact. It is also the area of greatest public concern, since it is so new. Without a rich base of experience on which to draw, it is very difficult to say just how technology can be most effectively used in mathematics education. Fortunately, sufficient research has been done by pioneers in this field to suggest general trends and likely results.

The effects of calculators in school mathematics have been studied in over 100 formal investigations during the past 15 years. These studies have tested the impact of a variety of kinds of calculator use—from limited access in carefully selected situations to access for all aspects of mathematics instruction and testing. There have been two major summaries of research on calculator usage (Hembree and Dessart, 1986; Suydam, 1986). In almost every reported study, the performance of groups using calculators equaled or exceeded that of control groups denied calculator use.

The recent Hembree and Dessart meta-analysis of 79 calculator studies sorted out the effects of calculator use on six dimensions of attitude toward mathematics as well as on the acquisition, retention, and transfer of computational skill, conceptual understanding, and problem-solving ability. The analysis led to this conclusion (Hembree and Dessart, 1986):

> Students who use calculators in concert with traditional instruction maintain their paper-and-pencil skills without apparent harm. Indeed, use of calculators can improve the average student's basic skills with paper and pencil, both in basic operations and in problem solving.

Research suggests that access to calculators in a well-planned program of instruction is not likely to obstruct achievement of skill in traditional arithmetic procedures. More optimistically, it appears that when students have access to calculators for learning and achievement testing, they perform at significantly higher levels on both computation and problem solving. In particular, students using calculators seem better able to focus on correct analysis of problem situations.

The earliest educational use of computers was focused on computer-assisted instruction (CAI), often based on programmed learning, most frequently for drill on rote skills. Several reviews of research on the effectiveness of CAI (e.g., Bangert-Drowns et al., 1985) have concluded that it is generally very effective, giving better achievement in shorter time than traditional instruction.

Lately, principles of artificial intelligence have been applied to design of sophisticated tutors for algebra, geometry, and calculus. The designers suggest that the use of such tutors can yield dramatic increases in student achievement. However, no data are yet available about the use of such tutors in realistic classroom settings.

There are several kinds of computer-based systems that give students powerful new tools for learning in an exploratory environment. Best known is Logo; its turtle graphics teach students concepts of geometry, algebra, and higher-order thinking (Papert, 1980). Although research findings have failed to confirm the strongest claims that Logo develops a high level of general reasoning, a variety of studies have found positive effects on more specific instructional goals (Campbell, 1989). Moreover, thousands of classroom teachers have been convinced by first-hand experience that Logo is a powerful instructional tool.

A different sort of computer-based exploratory tool is provided by the Geometric Supposer (Schwartz and Yerushalmy, 1987) and Geodraw (Bell, 1987). Each provides students with open but guided environments for exploring the results of geometric constructions. Green Globs (Dugdale, 1982) provides a comparable setting for algebraic exploration. Although there is little formal research describing the effects of these learning

and teaching tools, there are some suggestions (Yerushalmy et al., 1987) that students may perform as well or better than control students on traditional criteria while at the same time learning other objectives.

Some investigators have studied the effects of computer graphics on student under-standing of mathematical con-cepts like function (Rhoads, 1986; Schoenfeld, 1988a) or statistics and data analysis (Swift, 1984). In each case, the computer seems clearly to enhance student interest and understanding of important ideas.

Although most studies have focused, one way or another, on finding better ways to reach traditional goals, there have been some daring departures from conventional curriculum priorities. Both Lesh (1987) and Heid and Kunkle (1988) tested the effects of experimental algebra instruction in which stu-dents used symbol manipulation software to perform routine tasks like solving equations. Each found that students who were freed from the traditional symbolic procedural aspects of problem solving became much more adept at problem for-mulation and interpretation.

In two similar studies of computer-aided calculus, Heid (1988) and Palmiter (1986) found that students who learned calculus with the aid of computer software developed a much deeper understanding of fundamental concepts than did students in traditional skill-oriented courses. Heid also found that her students picked up needed procedural knowledge in a short time period following careful instruction in conceptual background, and Palmiter found that her students acquired their understanding much more quickly than students in con-ventional courses.

Open Questions

Most current research addresses fundamental questions of technology applied to the mathematics curriculum: What are the essential interactions among conceptual development, procedural knowledge, and problem solving? This research indicates that access to computers and calculators need not hinder attainment of traditional curricular objectives, and that it may substantially advance it. Unfortunately, there is no consensus on how to investigate new effects such as the improvement of higher-order thinking skills. A series of articles in *Educational Researcher* (Becker, 1987; Papert, 1987; Pea, 1987b; Walker, 1987) illustrate the wide diversity of opinion on this topic. A key concern is the extent to which the development of mathematical power can be inferred from written test performance or within the limited time spans of most research studies.

It has sometimes been proposed that the availability of computers would, more or less in itself, produce significant improvements in mathematical thinking. From the few attempts that have been made to measure changes in reasoning power, it is possible to conclude that such advancements cannot come from trivial technological fixes. Repeated attempts to document such change has yet to reveal a lasting effect: for example, studies of the effect of Logo on planning, of the impact of Pascal on understanding of algebraic syntax, and of the cognitive impact of learning metaprinciples of programming in Basic. While these results do not necessarily imply that computers will not improve mathematical thinking, they do suggest that simplistic approaches are not likely to produce measurable improvements.

Rapid changes in the objectives and strategies of mathematics education have outpaced the evidence of effectiveness provided by educational research (NRC, 1985). Introduction of calculators and computers, especially, opens up many new issues that need careful study:

- *Organization for Learning.* Changes in curriculum, in teaching practice, and in the educational role of computers and calculators provide both opportunity and compelling need for new research on the effectiveness of different strategies. Computers virtually compel reordering and new combinations of traditional topics. What orders yield optimal learning?

- *Levels of Learning.* Technology makes possible earlier introduction of certain topics (e.g., decimals). What is the relation between the stage of introduction and ultimate understanding?

- *Modes of Learning.* As instruction recognizes an active role for students in constructing their own knowledge, we need to monitor the long-term impact of this approach on students' abilities to learn and to use mathematical concepts throughout their lives.

- *Manipulative Skills.* Powerful calculators compel reexamination of traditional priorities for arithmetic and algebraic skills. Which skills best support mathematical power, and when must they be taught?

- *Procedural and Conceptual Knowledge.* What level of manipulative skill is necessary in order to be able to understand—and thus use—mathematics in a problem-solving context?

- *Transfer of Knowledge.* How can school instruction provide students with a background that will enable them to apply what they have learned in out-of-school contexts?

- *Instructional Uses of Technology.* Technological research has just begun to create tools with the power to alter significantly the traditional process of instruction. What kinds of mathematical comprehension can these new tools foster?

Redesign from a Research Perspective

Recent international comparative studies indicate that some of our basic assumptions about the structure and goals of schooling, about children's abilities, and about the structure of curricula are determined more by tradition than by fundamental educational principles (Crosswhite et al., 1986). For example:

- Mothers of American children are far more likely than are mothers of Japanese and Taiwanese children to believe that innate ability underlies children's success in mathematics (Stevenson et al., 1986).

- The curricula of other countries reflect very different beliefs about what children are capable of learning. American textbooks tend to develop ideas very slowly by progressing through a hierarchy of small, straightforward learning tasks. Texts from Asian countries and from the Soviet Union immerse students in much more demanding problem situations from the beginning (Fuson et al., 1988).

- Mathematics classrooms in Japan use instructional time in quite different ways than American schools. For example, group work and cooperative problem solving are stressed throughout the earliest grades (Easley and Easley, 1982; Enloe and Lewin, 1987).

These comparisons underscore that schooling is a reflection of societal values, that we must think of "curriculum" in societal as well as in classroom terms. The emphasis on mathematics in Chinese and Japanese classrooms is a reflection of the importance that the Chinese and Japanese parents ascribe to mathematics learning.

The findings of international comparisons are confirmed by National Assessments of Educational Progress (Dossey et al., 1988). All studies consistently show disappointing levels of student performance in areas of mathematical power, understanding, and relevant applications. Performance is most disappointing in understanding and problem solving, the very aspects of mathematics most important for working and living in a technology-intensive society.

Learning Mathematics

These difficulties can be overcome only through new modes of teaching (Resnick, 1987). By synthesizing a broad range of observational research, Romberg and Carpenter (1986) document a curricular tradition in mathematics built on a massive record of knowledge divorced from science and other disciplines. Mathematics education, unlike mathematics itself, is separated into subjects and subdivided into topics, studies, lessons, facts, and skills. "This fragmentation of mathematics has divorced the subject from reality and from inquiry. Such essential characteristics of mathematics as abstracting, inventing, proving, and applying are often lost."

Research on teaching for higher-order thinking lends support to the notion that instruction needs to change from the traditional mode where the teacher presents material to a less structured, more indirect style of teaching (Dessart and Suydam, 1983; Grouws et al., 1988; Peterson, 1988; Peterson and Carpenter, 1989). Because the development of higher-level thinking in mathematics depends on autonomous, independent learning behavior, teachers (and parents) must learn how to encourage more self-reliance in students who are learning mathematics.

Explicit teaching of cognitive and metacognitive strategies can enhance students' learning (Schoenfeld, 1987), as can small group cooperative learning (Shavelson et al., 1988; Peterson and Carpenter, 1989). Cognitive research in other content areas (Campione et al., 1988) shows the effectiveness of reciprocal teaching in which children take turns playing teacher, posing questions, summarizing, clarifying, and predicting. Reciprocal teaching is based on the premise that the opportunity to construct meanings communally internalizes the process and gives these constructions permanence (Resnick, 1988).

Constructed Knowledge

There is now wide agreement among researchers (Resnick, 1983; Linn, 1986) of the need to pay careful attention to student-constructed knowledge (Piaget, 1954). For example, Resnick (1976), Carpenter et al. (1982), and Steffe et al. (1983) have shown that when adding two numbers, say 3 + 6, students generally invent the method of counting on (that is, "7, 8, 9"). Children come to school with a rich body of knowledge about the world around them, including well-developed informal systems of mathematics (Ginsburg, 1977). Education fails when children are treated as "blank slates" or "empty jugs," ignoring the fact that they have a great deal of mathematical knowledge, some of which surpasses—and some of which may contradict—what they are being taught in school (Erlwanger, 1974; Clement, 1977; Gelman and Gallistal, 1978; Ginsburg, 1983).

Children are active interpreters of the world around them, including the mathematical aspects of that world. In the words of Piaget (1948), "To understand is to invent." Topics in school should be arranged to exploit intuitions and informal numerical notions that students bring with them to school. Moreover, teaching methods must adapt to the notion of the child as interpreter and constructor of (possibly wrong) theories as opposed to the child as absorber.

Thinking Visually

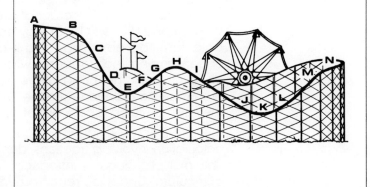

Here is a picture of a roller-coaster track:
Sketch a graph to show the speed of the roller coaster versus its position on the track.

Procedural Knowledge

The recommendation to reduce emphasis on procedures used for paper-and-pencil calculations rests in part on extensive evidence that these procedures, in themselves, do not aid conceptual understanding (Mestre, 1987). The literature on arithmetic "bugs" (Brown and Burton, 1978; Maurer, 1987) reveals that many mistakes students make follow predictable patterns. Such consistent but mistaken procedures—learning bugs—have a natural origin in the invention of the student: they are intelligent attempts to modify memorized procedures that are poorly understood.

Even when correctly learned, purely procedural knowledge—the ability to implement mathematical algorithms without underlying conceptual knowledge—can be extremely fragile. Clement et al. (1979) have shown that even a solid procedural knowledge of algebra, such as is held by university-level engineering students, does not in most cases (over 80%) imply an ability to interpret the meaning of algebraic symbols. Several recent studies show that mathematical learning is more robust when taught in a fashion that stresses underlying conceptual models (e.g., Carpenter et al., 1982; Davis, 1984; Hiebert, 1986; Romberg and Carpenter, 1986).

Mastery of Subject Matter

Mastery of subject matter has for years been the predominant focus of mathematics education research. Yet researchers have only just begun to construct a detailed map of the phases children can go through as they build understanding of arithmetic (Steffe et al., 1983). Even at early ages, the picture is quite complex. Contrary to much present practice, it is generally most effective to engage students in meaningful, complex activities focusing on conceptual issues rather than to establish all building blocks at one level before going on to the next level (Hatano, 1982; Romberg and Carpenter, 1986; Collins et al., 1989).

In certain cases, the order of presentation appears critical. Wearne and Hiebert (1988) showed that students who learn to calculate too early may find it more difficult to reach an understanding than students who have had no such experience. On the other hand, Steffe et al. (1983) showed that children must be able to recite the number words in order before they can develop a concept of counting or number.

There is some evidence to suggest that paper and pencil calculation involving fractions, decimal long division, and possibly multiplication are introduced far too soon in the present curriculum. Under currently prevalent teaching practice, a very high percentage of high school students worldwide never masters these topics—just what one would expect in a case where routinized skills are blocking semantic learning (e.g., Benezet, 1935). The challenge for curriculum development (and research) is to determine when routinized rules should come first and when they should not, as well as to investigate newer whole-language strategies for teaching that may be more effective than traditional methods. This is an area where far more research needs to be done.

Problem Solving

Problem solving is a central focus of the mathematics curriculum. There is by now an extensive body of literature (Krulik, 1980; Mason et al., 1982; Schoenfeld, 1985; Silver, 1985; Charles and Silver, 1988; Noddings, 1988) indicating that strategies for problem solving can be taught effectively. The main warning from the research literature is that one should be careful not to trivialize problem-solving strategies, teaching a collection of isolated tricks (e.g., "of" means multiply, or cross-cancelling factors). Problem-solving strategies, in the spirit of Polya (1945), are subtle and complex. Important strategies such as "look for a pattern by plugging in values for $n = 1, 2, 3, 4, \ldots$" cannot be taught effectively apart from the situational clues that indicate when such strategies are appropriate. For a nice collection of "starter" problems and a discussion of mathematical thinking, see Mason et al. (1982). For a discussion of problem posing (as opposed to mere problem solving), see Brown and Walter (1983).

An effective approach to solving problems is provided by metacognition, the self-conscious ability to know when and why to use a procedure. There is ample evidence (Schoenfeld, 1985; Silver, 1985; Campione et al., 1988; Collins et al., 1989) that students who know more than enough subject matter often fail to solve problems because they do not use their knowledge wisely. They may jump into problems, doggedly pursuing a particular ill-chosen approach to the exclusion of anything else; they may raise profitable alternatives, but fail to pursue them; they may get side-tracked into focusing on trivia while ignoring the "big picture."

Research indicates that such "executive" skills can be learned, resulting in significant improvements in problem-solving performance. Effects can be obtained with interventions as simple as holding class discussions that focus on executive behaviors, and by explicitly and frequently posing questions such as: "What are you doing?" "Why are you doing it?" "How will it help you?"

Making Sense of Mathematics

The current curriculum fails badly in teaching genuine applications of mathematics (Dossey et al., 1988). In a report of the Third National Assessment of Educational Progress (Carpenter et al., 1983), nearly 30% of children reported the answer of "31 remainder 12" to the problem:

> An Army bus holds 36 soldiers. If 1128 soldiers are being bused to their training site, how many buses are needed?

Fewer than one in four gave the correct answer to the problem. Approximately 70 percent of the students who took the examination performed the right operation (1128 divided by 36 yields "31 remainder 12"). However, fewer than one-third of those students checked "32 buses" as their answer. Many students extract from their school experience the general view that the result of an algorithm (e.g., "31 remainder 12") is the correct and complete answer. Very little in their experience would suggest the need to interpret the result of a mathematical procedure.

For most students, school mathematics is a habit of problem-solving without sense-making: one learns to read the problem, to extract the relevant numbers and the operation to be used, to perform the operation, and to write down the result—without ever thinking about what it all means.

Reusser (1986) reports that three school children in four will produce a numerical answer to nonsense problems such as:

> There are 125 sheep and 5 dogs in a flock. How old is the shepherd?

Typical responses, produced by a student solving the problem out loud, exemplify the mindless world of school mathematics:

> 125 + 5 = 130 . . . this is too big, and 125 - 5 = 120 is still too big . . . while 125/5 = 25. That works. I think the shepherd is 25 years old.

Students constantly strive to make sense of the rules that govern the world around them, including the world of their mathematics classrooms. If the classroom patterns are perceived to be arbitrary and the mathematical operations meaningless—no matter how well "mastered" as procedures—students will emerge from the classroom with a sense of mathematics as being arbitrary, useless, and meaningless.

The classroom culture in which students learn mathematics shapes their understanding of the nature of mathematics as well as the ways they will use the mathematics they have learned. Many studies (Fawcett, 1938; Bruner, 1964; Mason et al., 1982; Burton, 1984; Lave et al., 1988; Schoenfeld, 1988b) indicate that it is indeed possible to create classroom environments that are, in essence, cultures of sense-making—cultures from which students emerge with an understanding of mathematics as a discipline that helps to make sense of things. The goal of teaching sense-making via mathematics should be a central concern of all curricular reform.

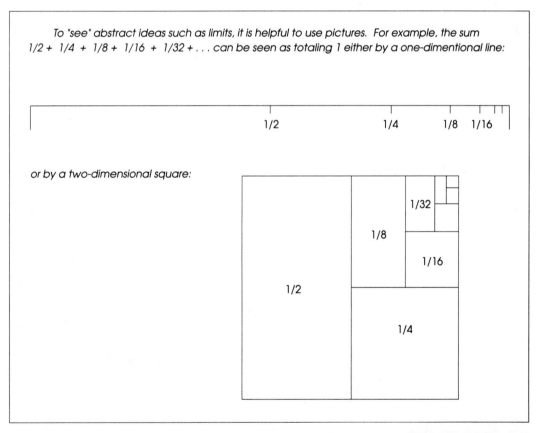

To "see" abstract ideas such as limits, it is helpful to use pictures. For example, the sum 1/2 + 1/4 + 1/8 + 1/16 + 1/32 + . . . can be seen as totaling 1 either by a one-dimentional line:

1/2   1/4   1/8   1/16

or by a two-dimensional square:

1/2   1/4   1/8   1/16   1/32

Proofs Without Words

A Framework for Change

Curriculum discussions always involve, implicitly if not explicitly, many different curricula of progressively diminishing scope:

- An *expected* curriculum, that represents future needs of employers and science.

- An *ideal* curriculum, that establishes actual goals for teaching and learning.

- An *available* curriculum, that can be taught with existing teaching materials and currently trained teachers.

- An *adopted* curriculum, that a school district says should be taught.

- An *implemented* curriculum, that teachers actually teach.

- An *assessed* curriculum, that is examined by tests or other forms of evaluation.

- An *achieved* curriculum, that most students actually master.

A major aim of curriculum development should be to close the gap between the expected and the achieved curricula. To do this, one must make the gaps between each pair of successive steps in the hierarchy as small as possible. There are, however, no unique curricula that will do this. We aim, therefore, to provide a framework within which many curricula may bloom.

Principles

Pressure to reshape mathematics education comes from many directions—from technology, from society, from research, and from mathematics itself. The broad practical view of mathematics as a science and language of patterns provides a strong foundation for new mathematics curricula. Technological change and research findings suggest directions for curricular change. Such change will take many forms, but should be built on certain fundamental principles that follow from our view of mathematics and our review of research.

Principle 1: Mathematics education must focus on the development of mathematical power.

Mathematical power enables students to understand mathematical concepts and methods and to discern mathematical relations in a variety of contexts. It helps students to reason logically and to solve a variety of problems, both routine and nonroutine. To be effective,

mathematical power requires of students that they be able to read documents using mathematical methods and express quantitative and logical analyses in both oral and written form.

Students who achieve significant mathematical power during their school years will be able to use mathematics in their careers and in everyday lives. They will be intelligent users of mathematical ideas, accepting or rejecting claims that are ostensibly based on mathematical arguments. They will see things mathematically, recognizing when mathematical analyses help to explain events. They will have sufficient mathematical knowledge to pursue a profession or vocation of their choice and to undertake further study of subjects that require mathematical proficiency.

Mathematical power entails the capability to communicate about mathematics. In addition to learning how to solve problems, students must also learn to read and understand mathematical texts and to express to others both orally and in writing the results of mathematical investiga-

tions and problem solving. The mathematics curriculum, therefore, must provide appropriate contexts in which students can learn to read, write, and speak about mathematics.

Principle 2: Calculators and computers should be used throughout the mathematics curriculum.

Students will achieve mathematical power only if they see mathematics as a modern, relevant subject. New curricular materials must be designed in the expectation of continuous change resulting from further scientific and technological developments. In mathematics, understanding cannot generally be achieved without active participation in the actual process of mathematics—in conjecture and argument, in exploration and reasoning, in formulating and solving, in calculation and verification. Calculators function like "fast pencils," so the mathematical process can be made more useful and efficient than with paper and pencil. Computers, similarly, enable students to quickly calculate, graph, or simulate processes that are simply impossible to carry out by any other means. Instruction based on calculators and computers has, therefore, the potential to lead to more understanding than does traditional instruction.

Calculators and computers also appeal to teachers because they introduce excitement and inventiveness to otherwise routine courses. Of course, technology should not be used just because it is appealing. But it must be used when it can enhance the teaching and learning of mathematics. There are very few portions of the curriculum where such improvement is not possible.

Principle 3: Relevant applications should be an integral part of the curriculum.

Students need to experience mathematical ideas in the context in which they naturally arise—from simple counting and measurement to applications in business and science. Calculators and computers make it possible now to introduce realistic applications throughout the curriculum.

The significant criterion for the suitability of an application is whether it has the potential to engage students' interests and stimulate their mathematical thinking. Appealing applications should be drawn from the world in which the child lives, from community events, or from other parts of the curriculum—and not just from science, but also from business, geography, art, and other subjects.

The primary goal of instruction should be for students to learn to use mathematical tools in contexts that mirror their use in actual situations. Mathematical ideas should always be presented and developed in the context of meaningful mathematical activities.

Principle 4: Each part of the curriculum should be justified on its own merits.

Mathematics offers such a rich array of interesting and useful ideas that choices are necessarily difficult. However, no concept or skill should remain in the curriculum just because it is there now. Although there is much that is timeless in the present curriculum, we can no longer afford as the chief justification for a topic that it is in the curriculum already. We need, instead, a "zero-based" curriculum process in which no idea is immune from careful scrutiny.

Revision of curriculum should not be just an exercise in adding more topics. It should be, rather, a discipline of establishing priorities. Some emphases should be dropped, others added, and some retained. Even for important priorities that do remain, modern applications or technology may suggest quite different approaches. Often a fresh approach can avoid the rigidity of thought that inhibits desirable change.

In many districts, the secondary mathematics curriculum especially is already full of topics, many treated too quickly. Nevertheless, there is much mathematics that could be made accessible and interesting to students. Unless traditional topics contribute directly to curricular goals, they clutter the curriculum. Neither the number of topics nor the nature of the topics is as important as a curriculum that instills in students firm command of mathematical thinking.

Principle 5: Curricular choices should be consistent with contemporary standards for school mathematics.

The new *Curriculum and Evaluation Standards for School Mathematics* (National Council of Teachers of Mathematics (NCTM), 1989) exemplify the kind of broad curricular standards that should be used as criteria for assessing the merit of topics in school mathematics. Similar standards are expressed in many recent state documents, for example, California (Denham and O'Malley, 1985) and Wisconsin (Chambers, 1986). Although differing in many details, these various documents establish significant new goals for effective school mathematics. Local choices should be made in a manner consistent with these curricular standards. The pace of change is so great that even current curriculum guides are likely to be inadequate for tomorrow's needs. Curricular change requires sustained effort by people of vision, rooted in the reality of schools, yet with objectives firmly set on the future.

Principle 6: Mathematics instruction at all levels should foster active student involvement.

The proper use of technology requires new approaches to teaching mathematics in which students will be much more active learners. Quite aside from technology, research on how students learn suggests more effective ways to teach mathematics. Mathematics teaching must adapt to both of these developments. It will no longer be appropriate for most mathematics instruction to be in the traditional mode where teachers present material to a class of passive students.

No single teaching method nor any single kind of learning experience can develop the varied mathematical abilities implied under the definition of mathematical power (Fey, 1979; Mathematical Sciences Education Board (MSEB), 1987). What is needed is a variety of activities, including discussion among pupils, practical work, practice of important techniques, problem solving, application of everyday situations, investigational work, and exposition by the teacher.

Teachers should be catalysts who help students learn to think for themselves. They should not act solely as trainers whose role is to show the "right way" to solve problems. In addition, classroom activities should provide ample opportunity for students to communicate with each other using the language of mathematics in both written and oral form.

A useful metaphor is that of the teacher as an intellectual coach. At various times, this will require that the teacher be:

- A *role model* who demonstrates not just the right way, but also the false starts and higher-order thinking skills that lead to the solution of problems;

- A *consultant* who helps individuals, small groups, or the whole class to decide if their work is keeping to the subject and making reasonable progress;

- A *moderator* who poses questions to consider, but leaves much of the decision making to the class;

- An *interlocutor* who supports students during class presentations, encouraging them to reflect on their activities and to explore mathematics on their own;

- A *questioner* who challenges students to make sure that what they are doing is reasonable and purposeful, and ensures that students can defend their conclusions.

All these roles serve well the most important aim of education, namely, to wean students from their teachers. Mathematics education must aim to make students self-sufficient, so that they can use mathematics effectively without a teacher present, as they must once they leave the school environment. To do this, schools must foster sufficient independence in students that they can function mathematically on their own while still in school, or there will be no possibility of their doing so after leaving school.

Goals

By themselves, general principles provide insufficient direction to help focus curriculum development. More specific goals, related to the new *Curriculum and Evaluation Standards for School Mathematics* (NCTM, 1989), must be built on the foundation provided by our expression of a practical philosophy of mathematics as a language and science of patterns, and on the related technological and research perspectives. These goals offer a more constructive framework for the process of curricular change.

Mathematics education needs to be viewed as an integrated whole, progressing continually from primary school through graduate school. Students learn in different ways and at different rates, in different directions and at different depths. Such differences cut across grade levels and school-level boundaries. Many areas of mathematics, not just arithmetic, algebra, and geometry, should be seen as lengthy strands to be woven throughout all of school mathematics.

Notwithstanding the continuity of mathematics, goals for different levels of school must reflect different stages in children's development of mathematical power. As new curricula are developed to meet the challenges of a changing society, they must strive to achieve certain broad goals that form an effective framework for school mathematics:

A primary goal of elementary school mathematics is to develop number sense.

Student abilities to reason effectively with numerical information requires experience with:

- *Representation*—the ability to use numbers to express quantitative data and relations.

- *Operations*—mastery of single-digit arithmetic; ability to determine appropriate arithmetic procedures; facility in estimation; experience in selecting appropriate means to carry out complex calculations.

- *Interpretation*—the ability to draw inferences from data and check both the data and the inferences for accuracy and reasonableness.

Elementary school mathematics should use concrete materials, computer software, and calculators. It should emphasize mental arithmetic, particularly for estimating the results of multidigit computations. At the same time there should be a sharp reduction in time devoted to teaching the traditional written methods of calculation for multidigit numbers, fractions, and decimals.

An elementary school curriculum that approaches arithmetic from this perspective will be strikingly different from the arithmetic commonly taught today. The central mathematical task of today's elementary school is to develop manual skill in a wide variety of operations on whole numbers, rational fractions, and decimals. Reducing emphasis on these topics while increasing opportunities for reasoning, for discovering patterns, for identifying correct procedures, and for drawing inferences will require a fundamental change in the conditions of teaching. A school mathematics program with this kind of emphasis offers the promise of impressive progress in the level of quantitative reasoning.

Elementary school mathematics should provide an effective foundation for all aspects of mathematics.

If students are to be better prepared mathematically for vocations as well as for everyday life, the elementary school mathematics must include substantial subject matter other than arithmetic:

- *Geometry,* including properties of two- and three-dimensional objects, symmetry and congruence, constructions of geometric figures, and transformations of geometric figures;

- *Measurement,* including units of measure, telling time, reading temperatures, and computing with money;

- *Data analysis,* including collection, organization, representation, and interpretation of data; construction of statistical tables and diagrams; and the use of data for analytic and predictive purposes;

- *Probability,* introduced with simple experiments and data-gathering;

- *Discrete mathematics,* including basic combinatorial thinking and the use of graphs to model problems.

Each of these topics can play a distinctive role in making the elementary school mathematics curriculum more interesting and relevant to students. Geometry provides an obvious window on the physical world, now enhanced through computer graphics. In mathematics as in life, a picture is worth a thousand words. Measurement provides meaningful applications even to very young children, as well as reinforcement of number concepts. Data analysis provides a source of interesting and relevant problems, as does probability, which can also be related to familiar games. Concepts from algebra can introduce students to simple aspects of abstraction, while discrete mathematics provides topics to relate mathematics to many areas, particularly computers.

Moreover, instruction should be integrated so that relations among different areas will be perceived and reinforced. For example, teachers should stress the use of arithmetic in geometry and probability, and the use of geometric concepts in the representation of data.

Calculators should be available in all instructional and assessment situations.

Calculators should be used in school mathematics from kindergarten on as devices that children use to develop and discover number relationships and to solve problems. The replacement of most paper-and-pencil drills with calculator-based instruction will not itself be a panacea. Although it is just as possible to assign mindless drills with calculators as with paper and pencil, young children can instead be given activities with calculators that emphasize discovery and exploration in ways not possible or practical with paper and pencil.

It is as important as ever for children to learn when and how to use addition, subtraction, multiplication, and division. But there is no evidence that drill-and-practice on standard algorithms leads to understanding. Mathematics educators must take advantage of calculator-based instruction as a tool to help students to achieve this understanding.

Students learning mathematics should use real objects and real data.

Observation is as fundamental to mathematics as to science. Young children need to manipulate real objects as they learn to count and to explore arithmetic. To develop sound intuition for length, area, volume, and shape, children studying mathematics must draw, cut, fold, construct, pour, and measure.

Children of all ages must constantly explore the relation between the relatively pristine patterns studied in school mathematics and the messier reality of worldly data. Real data are more convincing than contrived data. The act of gathering data—whether by measurement, counting, polls, experiments, or computer simulation—enriches the child's engagement in learning. Moreover, the inevitable dialogue that emerges between the reality of measurement and the reality of calculation—between the experimental and the theoretical—captures the whole science of mathematics.

Middle school mathematics should emphasize the practical power of mathematics.

If instruction is to give students mathematical power, then problem solving needs to be emphasized throughout all grades. Students need to perceive mathematics as more than the subject matter itself—as, in fact, a discipline of reasoning that enables them to attack and solve problems of increasing difficulty and complexity. A focus on problems rather than just on exercises is important throughout the curriculum.

Broadening the elementary school curriculum has important implications about entry into secondary school mathematics. The middle school grades should not be viewed as a time for consolidation or as a pause for rest, but as an essential part of a child's mathematical development. Its focus should be on mathematics for everyday life, a theme rich in motivation that leads naturally to many important mathematical topics (e.g., data analysis, geometric measurement, interest rates, and spreadsheet analysis). Understanding the concepts of elementary school mathematics is essential for the study of secondary school mathematics; however, proficiency in the procedures of hand arithmetic computation should no longer be the critical factor in judging student readiness for advanced study.

Mathematics in school should reinforce other school subjects, and vice versa.

Much of the motivation for the development of mathematics—both historical and personal—is related to science, yet in school there are precious few honest links between mathematics and any of its applications. The applications of mathematics extend far beyond the natural sciences—to business, social science, geography, and various vocational and commercial areas. Young children can learn much mathematics in the context of explorations: experience with data, practice with arithmetic, and exposure to shapes and change. High school students need to experience applications in their mathematics classes as well as to use mathematics extensively in other classes.

Since mathematics is both the language of science and a science of patterns, the special links between mathematics and science are far more than just those between theory and applications. The methodology of mathematical inquiry shares with the scientific method a focus on exploration, investigation, conjecture, evidence, and reasoning. Firmer school ties between science and mathematics should especially help strengthen students' grasp of both fields.

A major goal of the secondary mathematics curriculum should be to develop symbol sense.

The transition from elementary to secondary mathematics is characterized by a shift from concrete objects to abstract symbols. Developing fluency with symbols and other abstract entities—which can be geometric, algebraic, or algorithmic—must be a central aim of secondary school mathematics. Student ability to reason effectively with symbols requires experience with:

- *Representation*—the ability to represent mathematical problems in symbolic form and to use these symbolic representations in relations, expressions, and equations;

- *Operations*—the ability to determine appropriate symbolic procedures and to select appropriate means to solve problems expressed in symbolic form;

- *Interpretation*—the ability to draw inferences by reasoning with symbolic systems to check these results for accuracy and reasonableness.

Computers and calculators have, of course, an important role to play in the development of symbol sense. Since powerful calculators will have just as profound an effect on how symbolic manipulations are done as they have had on how arithmetic is done, the current emphasis in secondary school on manipulative skills will need to be replaced by a larger emphasis on understand-

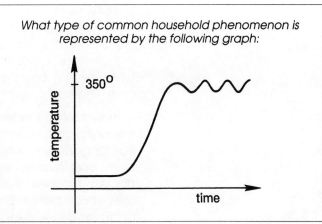

ing and problem solving. A valuable impact of technology on the secondary curriculum will surely be the development of sophisticated software that will enable students to discover patterns rather than just to manipulate symbols.

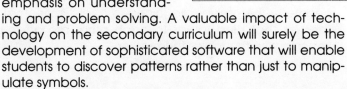

Mystery Graph

Secondary school mathematics should introduce the entire spectrum of mathematical sciences.

Secondary school mathematics must prepare students for the workplace, for college, and for citizenship. To meet these objectives, the curriculum must include a broad range of topics reflecting the full power of the mathematical sciences:

- *Algebra,* including general algorithms and families of functions (polynomial, trigonometric, exponential, logarithmic).

- *Geometry,* including transformational geometry, vector geometry, solid geometry, and analytic geometry.

- *Data analysis,* including measures of uncertainty, probability and sampling distributions, and inferential reasoning.

- *Discrete mathematics,* including combinatorics, graph theory, recurrence relations, and recursion—all emphasizing algorithmic thinking.

- *Optimization,* including mathematical modelling, "what if" analysis, systems thinking, and network flows.

Stressing general algorithms in a computer context will make algebra and trigonometry more interesting. Despite its reputation as a subject that is boring and irrelevant, geometry has always been a subject of great potential interest because of its associations with the physical world. Data analysis can easily be related to interesting and significant applications, as can discrete mathematics and optimization.

In teaching mathematics it is important to illustrate the unity and integrity of the discipline. For example, fractal geometry is quite accessible to high school students and involves aspects of algebra, geometry, and discrete mathematics, as well as providing fascinating uses of computers. Data analysis leads directly to algebraic and geometric methods, while algebra and geometry themselves are joined in analytic geometry. The ties that bind topics to each other are often as important as the topics themselves.

Students should apprehend that in mathematics, reasoning is the standard of truth.

Learning to understand and construct logical, coherent mathematical arguments is a major goal of school mathematics. Euclidean geometry, however, is not the only vehicle for teaching students about reasoning. Both algebra and discrete mathematics provide excellent opportunities for arguments expressed in paragraph form; even flowcharts and spreadsheets can be used to illustrate the logical nature of mathematical argument.

More important than facility with formal proof is an understanding rooted in a variety of elementary examples that mathematical truth is logical and not purely empirical. Young children can develop a sense of logic from primitive experiences with numbers. Once symbols are understood, many basic ideas can be proved, often in a variety of ways. Geometric proofs of algebraic results (e.g., demonstrations of the Pythagorean formula by rearrangement of squares) are especially convincing to children who are still struggling to understand symbolic expressions.

All students should study mathematics every year they are in school.

Mathematics should play an important role in the education of all students, not only of those preparing for college. The core of secondary school mathematics should be fundamentally the same for all students, although the depth of presentation may vary. Enrichment beyond the core would naturally be differentiated to take into account the differing aspirations and probable further education of students. Students can learn to apply mathematics—indeed, they can often learn new mathematics—in other subjects (e.g., science, geography, business) provided appropriate links are forged between mathematics and these other disciplines. Mathematics, like writing, is a subject that should be regularly taught "across the curriculum."

Advocating that all students take essentially the same core mathematics may appear unrealistic, given the uneven preparation students bring to high school mathematics. Indeed, the United States separates students by ability earlier—and into more tracks—than any other industrialized country. Many students, under this system, are tracked out of real secondary school mathematics, being relegated to dead-end courses like "general mathematics." Too little has been expected for too long from too many students. Recognizing this, many give up much too early on studying significant amounts of mathematics in secondary school. More must be expected of our students than is the case now. Heightened expectation will surely lead to better performance.

All high schools should offer four full years of mathematics appropriate for all students. It is particularly important for students to take mathematics throughout their last year of high school. All too often, mathematics students who complete all of the mathematics available to them in the eleventh grade find that a year away from mathematics leaves them ill-prepared for college mathematics or for job-related requirements.

Enabling Conditions

One cannot separate curriculum and instruction from the broader context of education. To improve mathematics education, change must occur simultaneously in curriculum, in teaching, in professional development, in textbooks, and in assessment practices. Although our focus in this *Framework* is principally on the content of the curriculum, there are important implications of our recommendations for other parts of the educational context.

Professional Development
No significant curriculum reform will be possible without an effective program of professional development for mathematics teachers. As teachers implement important, timely, and exciting changes, they will require continuing programs of professional support. Such programs will require a commitment from local school districts as well as leadership and funding at the state and federal levels.

Although the evidence is more anecdotal than analytical, it is likely that many elementary school teachers would welcome an opportunity to increase their confidence about teaching mathematics. Increased confidence would encourage alternative styles of teaching that diminish emphasis on formalism and drill-and-practice. Any curriculum developed according to this framework will be more challenging to teach than the present curriculum. Therefore, particular attention must be paid to in-service training of elementary school teachers, as well as to the use of specialist mathematics teachers throughout the elementary school grades.

Secondary and middle school teachers who are already prepared to some extent with a specialization in mathematics will need extensive continuing education both in new areas of content that are not part of their present repertoire, and in styles of teaching better suited to active student participation. Programs that provide vertical integration of teaching, learning, and research experiences are well suited to this purpose since they enable teachers to experience for themselves the kind of open environment for learning that they should attempt to create for their students.

However, neither specialist teachers nor special programs to introduce a new curriculum can by themselves ensure success. Mathematics teachers, like other professionals, must engage in life-long programs of professional development. As professionals who must keep up with a rapidly changing and technically complex field, mathematics teachers especially need time and opportunity to read, to reflect, to plan, and to exchange ideas with other mathematics teachers. Furthermore, for teachers to succeed with a technology-based curriculum, they will need properly equipped classrooms and appropriate rewards for the special effort and innovative teaching that will be required. Teachers' working environments must support teachers' professional lives: an improved professional climate for teachers is absolutely critical for improvement in mathematics education.

Instructional Materials

In the overwhelming majority of classrooms, the content of the textbook determines what is taught and how it is taught. Teachers may skip topics in textbooks, but they will seldom give significant attention to topics not included in texts. Neither will most teachers approach a topic differently from the way it is treated in the text. Therefore, real curriculum change is possible only if it is accompanied by new curricular materials.

New textbooks must be designed and written to reflect the important principles of mathematics curricula: genuine problems; calculators and computers; relevant applications; reading and writing about mathematics; and active strategies for learning. It is not sufficient for publishers to provide ancillary software or supplementary materials to be used with a textbook but that are not discussed in it. Neither will it be acceptable to relegate new material to separate sections.

Publishers need to assess the entire structure and philosophy of current textbooks in light of research findings on how children construct mathematical images and how they learn to make sense of formal procedures. If textbooks began to integrate relevant insights from cognitive research, they would begin to exert a positive influence for change in school mathematics. Publishers also need to recognize that mathematics education will undergo significant and continuous change well into the next century. As a consequence, textbooks will become out-of-date more rapidly than in the past. This shortening of the useful life of a textbook will require considerable adjustment in publishers' plans and in school districts' purchase policies.

Textbooks must reflect fully a new conception of mathematics education, integrating into the main subject matter of the text all important principles of mathematics curricula and educational research. Unless textbooks help teachers to use actively calculators, computers, and genuine problems, new emphases such as technology and applications will continue to have insignificant impact on the curriculum. Unless textbooks contain engaging projects and group activities, few teachers will have time to create them on their own. And unless textbooks include suitable assignments to enhance students' experience with reading and writing in the language of mathematics, students will remain deficient in their ability to communicate effectively.

Assessment

Textbooks circumscribe what topics may be taught, but tests determine what topics will be taught. Too many of today's standardized tests stray far from both the available and the adopted curriculum; none even gets near the ideal curriculum. Just as new text materials must be developed in parallel with the new curriculum, so also should new strategies of and standards for assessment be developed as the curriculum is defined.

A curriculum fitting this framework will require methods of assessment quite different from current ones. Guidelines for effective assessment are discussed in the *Curriculum and Evaluation Standards for School Mathematics* (NCTM, 1989). Assessment must shape and guide instruction and not remain separate from it; it must determine not just what students do not know, but what they do know and how they think. Diagnostic materials that probe student understanding can provide a springboard for improved instruction. Assessment must permit full use of calculators and, where appropriate, of computers. Instruments can be developed to assess mathematical power rather than merely mathematical skill. But just as careful assessment of writing cannot be accomplished without having students write real essays, neither can mathematical power be assessed unless students have to solve nonroutine problems.

Mathematics for the Future

We are entering a decade in mathematics education of transition from entrenched precomputer traditions to new structures appropriate to the twenty-first century. These transitions will include:

- Greater breadth of mathematical sciences.
- More students who take more mathematics.
- Increased use of technology.
- More active learning.
- Enhanced professionalism for teachers.
- Increased need for higher-order thinking skills.
- More sophisticated means of assessment.

Effective change requires significant movement in each area, coordinated and sustained for an indefinite period. Efforts to orchestrate this change have only just begun, but must be continued.

The tapestry of mathematics in the twenty-first century will be woven not just from the ancient threads of algebra and geometry, but also from more contemporary themes such as uncertainty, symmetry, data, algorithm, and computation. As applications expand the variety of roles played by mathematics, and as computers reduce the role of routine calculations, the balance and connections among different parts of mathematics will change significantly.

Important threads in the tapestry extend throughout the entire range of the mathematics curriculum, providing rich opportunity for sustained development of a child's mathematical intuition and power. They lead to deep themes of contemporary mathematics; they point to ideas that explain and unify the process of mathematical discovery; and they provide a secure base for mathematics' many applications. The challenge for those who develop new mathematics curricula is to emphasize themes that both advance the power of mathematics and at the same time offer developmental opportunity for children's mathematical education.

References

Alligood, Bob (Ed.). *Improving Mathematics, Science, and Computer Education in Florida: A Comprehensive Plan.* Tallahasse: Florida Education and Industry Coalition, 1989.

American Association for the Advancement of Science. *Science for All Americans.* Washington, D.C.: American Association for the Advancement of Science, 1989.

Bangert-Drowns, R.; Kulik, J.A.; and Kulik, Chen C. "Effectiveness of Computer-Based Education in Secondary Schools." *Journal of Computer-Based Education,* 12:3 (Summer 1985), 59-68.

Becker, H.J. "The Importance of a Methodology that Maximizes Falsifiability: Its Applicability to Research about LOGO." *Educational Researcher,* 16:5 (1987), 11-16.

Bell, Max S. "Microcomputer-Based Courses for School Geometry." In Izaak Wirszup and Robert Streit (Eds.). *Developments in School Mathematics Education Around the World.* Reston, Va.: National Council of Teachers of Mathematics, 1987, 604-622.

Benezet, L.P. "The Story of an Experiment." *Teaching of Arithmetic,* 24 (1935), 8-9; 25; (1936), 1.

Board on Mathematical Sciences. *Mathematical Sciences: A Unifying and Dynamic Resource.* Washington, D.C.: National Academy Press, 1986.

Brown, J.S., and Burton, R.R. "Diagnostic Models for Procedural Bugs in Basic Mathematical Skills." *Cognitive Science,* 2 (1978), 155-192.

Brown, Stephen, and Walter, Marion. *The Art of Problem Posing.* Philadelphia, Pa.: The Franklin Institute Press, 1983.

Bruner, Jerome S. *On Knowing: Essays for the Left Hand.* Cambridge, Mass.: Belknap Press, 1964.

Burton, Leone. "Mathematical Thinking: The Struggle for Meaning." *Journal for Research in Mathematics Education,* 15:4 (January 1984), 35-49.

Campbell, Patricia F. "Young Children's Concept of Measure." In Leslie P. Steffe (Ed.). *Transforming Early Childhood Mathematics Education.* Hillsdale, N.J.: Lawrence Erlbaum Associates, 1989.

Campione, Joseph C.; Brown, Ann L.; and Connell, Michael L. "Metacognition: On the Importance of Understanding What You are Doing." In Randall I. Charles and Edward A. Silver (Eds.). *The Teaching and Assessing of Mathematical Problem Solving.* Reston, Va.: National Council of Teachers of Mathematics, 1988, 93-114.

Carpenter, Thomas. P.; Moser, J.; and Romberg, Thomas A. (Eds.). *Addition & Subtraction: A Cognitive Perspective.* Hillsdale, N.J.: Lawrence Erlbaum Associates, 1982.

Carpenter, Thomas P.; Lindquist, Mary M.; Matthews, W.; and Silver, Edward A. "Results of the Third NAEP Mathematics Assessment: Secondary School." *Mathematics Teacher,* 76:9 (December 1983), 652-659.

Chambers, Donald L. *A Guide to Curriculum Planning in Mathematics.* Madison: Wisconsin Department of Public Instruction, 1986.

Charles, Randall I., and Silver, Edward A. (Eds.). *The Teaching and Assessing of Mathematical Problem Solving.* Reston, Va.: National Council of Teachers of Mathematics, 1988.

Clement, J. "Quantitative Problem Solving Processes in Children." Ed.D. Dissertation, University of Massachusetts, Amherst, May 1977.

Clement, J.; Lockhead, J.; and Monk, G. "Translation Difficulties in Learning Mathematics." *American Mathematical Monthly,* 88 (1979), 4.

Collins, A.; Brown, J.S.; and Newman, S. "The New Apprenticeship: Teaching Students the Craft of Reading, Writing, and Mathematics." In D. Klahr (Ed.). *Cognition and Instruction: Issues and Agendas.* Hillsdale, N.J.: Lawrence Erlbaum Associates, 1989.

Conference Board of the Mathematical Sciences. "The Mathematical Sciences Curriculum K-12: What Is Still Fundamental and What Is Not." *In Educating Americans for the 21st Century: Source Materials.* National Science Board Commission on Precollege Education in Mathematics, Science, and Technology. Washington, D.C.: National Science Foundation, 1983, 1-23.

Crosswhite, F. Joe; Dossey, John A.; Swafford, Jane O.; McKnight, Curtis C.; Cooney, Thomas J.; Downs, Floyd L.; Grouws, Douglas A.; and Weinzweig, A.I. *Second International Mathematics Study: Detailed Report for the United States.* Champaign, Ill.: Stipes Publishing Company, 1986.

Davis, Robert B. *Learning Mathematics: The Cognitive Science Approach to Mathematics Education.* Norwood, N.J.: Ablex Publishing, 1984.

Denham, Walter F., and O'Malley, Edward T. (Eds.). *Mathematics Framework for California Public Schools, Kindergarten Through Grade Twelve.* Sacramento, Calif: California State Department of Education, 1985.

Dessart, Donald J., and Suydam, Marilyn N. *Classroom Ideas from Research on Secondary School Mathematics.* Reston, Va.: National Council of Teachers of Mathematics, 1983.

Dossey, John A.; Mullis, Ina V.S.; Lindquist, Mary M.; and Chambers, Donald L. *The Mathematics Report Card: Are We Measuring Up? Trends and Achievement Based on the 1986 National Assessment of Educational Progress (NAEP).* Princeton, N.J.: Educational Testing Service, 1988.

Dugdale, Sharon. "Green Globs: A Microcomputer Application for Graphing of Equations." *Mathematics Teacher,* 75:3 (March 1982), 208-214.

Easley, J., and Easley, E. "Ichinensei: The Introduction to Quantity in a Japanese Elementary School." Technical Report, University of Illinois, 1982.

Enloe, W., and Lewin, P. "The Cooperative Spirit in Japanese Primary Education." *Educational Forum,* 51:3 (Spring 1987), 233-247.

Erlwanger, S.H. "Case Studies of Children's Conceptions of Mathematics." Ph.D. Dissertation, University of Illinois, Champaign-Urbana, 1974.

Fawcett, Harold P. *The Nature of Proof.* Thirteenth NCTM Yearbook. New York: Columbia University Teacher's College, Bureau of Publications, 1938.

Fey, James T. "Mathematics Teaching Today: Perspectives From Three National Surveys." *Mathematics Teacher,* 72:7 (October 1979), 490-504.

Fey, James T. (Ed.). *Computing and Mathematics: The Impact on Secondary School Curricula.* Reston, Va.: National Council of Teachers of Mathematics, 1984.

Fuson, Karen C.; Stigler, James W.; and Bartsch, Karen. "Grade Placement of Addition and Subtraction Topics in Japan, Mainland China, the Soviet Union, Taiwan, and the United States." *Journal for Research in Mathematics Education,* 19 (November 1988), 449-456.

Gelman, R., and Gallistal, C. *The Child's Understanding of Number.* Cambridge, Mass.: Harvard University Press, 1978.

Ginsburg, H.P. *Children's Arithmetic: How They Learn It & How You Teach It.* New York: Van Nostrand Reinhold, 1977.

Ginsburg, H.P. (Ed.). *The Development of Mathematical Thinking.* New York: Academic Press, 1983.

Grouws, Douglas A.; Cooney, Thomas J.; and Jones, Douglas (Eds.). *Perspectives on Research on Effective Mathematics Teaching.* Reston, Va.: National Council of Teachers of Mathematics, 1988.

Hansen, Viggo P. (Ed.). *Computers in Mathematics Education.* 1984 NCTM Yearbook. Reston, Va.: National Council of Teachers of Mathematics, 1984.

Hatano, G. "Learning to Add and Subtract: A Japanese Perspective." In T. Carpenter, J. Moser, and T. Romberg (Eds). *Addition & Subtraction: A Cognitive Perspective.* Hillsdale, N.J.: Lawrence Erlbaum Associates, 1982.

Heid, M.K. "Resequencing Skills and Concepts in Applied Calculus Using the Computer as a Tool." *Journal for Research in Mathematics Education,* 19:1 (January 1988), 3-25.

Heid, M.K., and Kunkle, D. "Computer Generated Tables: Tools for Concept Development in Elementary Algebra." *In The Ideas of Algebra, K-12.* 1988 NCTM Yearbook. Reston, Va.: National Council of Teachers of Mathematics, 1988, 170-177.

Hembree, R., and Dessart, D. "Effects of Hand-held Calculators in Precollege Mathematics Education: A Meta-analysis." *Journal for Research in Mathematics Education,* 17:2 (1986), 83-89.

Hiebert, J. (Ed.). *Conceptual and Procedural Knowledge: The Case of Mathematics.* Hillsdale, N.J.: Lawrence Erlbaum Associates, 1986.

Howson, Geoffrey, and Kahane, J.-P. (Eds.). *The Influence of Computers and Informatics on Mathematics and Its Teaching.* International Commission on Mathematical Instruction Study Series. Cambridge, Mass.: Cambridge University Press, 1986.

Johnston, William B., and Packer, Arnold E. (Eds.). *Workforce 2000: Work and Workers for the Twenty-First Century.* Indianapolis, Ind.: Hudson Institute, 1987.

Krulik, Stephen (Ed.). *Problem Solving in School Mathematics.* 1980 NCTM Yearbook. Reston, Va.: National Council of Teachers of Mathematics, 1980.

Lapointe, Archie E.; Mead, Nancy A.; and Phillips, Gary W. *A World of Differences: An International Assessment of Science and Mathematics.* Princeton, N.J.: Educational Testing Service, 1989.

Lave, Jean; Smith, Steve; and Butler, Michael. "Problem Solving as Everyday Practice." In Randall I. Charles and Edward A. Silver (Eds.). *The Teaching and Assessing of Mathematical Problem Solving.* Reston, Va.: National Council of Teachers of Mathematics, 1988, 61-81.

Lesh, Richard. "The Evolution of Problem Representations in the Presence of Powerful Conceptual Amplifiers." In C. Janvier (Ed.). *Problems of Representation in the Teaching and Learning of Mathematics.* Hillsdale, N.J.: Lawrence Erlbaum Associates, 1987, 197-206.

Linn, Marcia C. (Ed.). "Establishing a Research Base for Science Education: Challenges, Trends and Recommendations." Report of a National Conference held January 16-19, 1986, University of California, Berkeley, May 1986.

Mason, J.; Burton, L.; and Stacey, K. *Thinking Mathematically.* Reading, Mass.: Addison-Wesley, 1982.

Mathematical Sciences Education Board, National Research Council. *The Teacher of Mathematics: Issues for Today and Tomorrow.* Washington, D.C.: National Academy Press, 1987.

Maurer, Stephen B. "New Knowledge About Errors and New Views About Learners: What They Mean to Educators and More Educators Would Like to Know." In A. Schoenfeld (Ed.). *Cognitive Science and Mathematics Education.* Hillsdale, N.J.: Lawrence Erlbaum Associates, 1987, 165-187.

McKnight, Curtis C.; Crosswhite, F. Joe; Dossey, John A.; Kifer, Edward; Swafford, Jane O.; Travers, Kenneth J.; and Cooney, Thomas J. *The Underachieving Curriculum: Assessing U.S. School Mathematics from an International Perspective.* Champaign, Ill.: Stipes Publishing Company, 1987.

Mestre, Jose. "Why Should Mathematics and Science Teachers Be Interested in Cognitive Research Findings?" *Academic Connections,* The College Board (1987), 3-5, 8-11.

National Council of Teachers of Mathematics. *Curriculum and Evaluation Standards for School Mathematics.* Reston, Va.: National Council of Teachers of Mathematics, 1989.

National Research Council: Committee on Research in Mathematics, Science, and Technology Education. *Mathematics, Science, and Technology Education: A Research Agenda.* Washington, D.C.: National Academy Press, 1985.

National Research Council. *Everybody Counts: A Report to the Nation on the Future of Mathematics Education.* Washington, D.C.: National Academy Press, 1989.

Noddings, Nel. "Preparing Teachers to Teach Mathematical Problem Solving." In Randall I. Charles and Edward A. Silver (Eds.). *The Teaching and Assessing of Mathematical Problem Solving.* Reston, Va.: National Council of Teachers of Mathematics, 1988, 244-258.

Oaxaca, Jaime, and Reynolds, Ann W. *Changing America: The New Face of Science and Engineering.* Washington, D.C.: Task Force on Women, Minorities, and the Handicapped in Science and Technology, September 1988.

Office of Technology Assessment. *Educating Scientists and Engineers, Grade School to Grad School.* Washington, D.C.: Office of Technology Assessment, 1988.

Palmiter, J.R. "The Impact of a Computer Algebra System on College Calculus." Dissertation, Ohio State University, November 1986.

Papert, Seymour. *Mindstorms: Children, Computers, and Powerful Ideas.* New York: Basic Books, 1980.

Papert, Seymour. "Information Technology and Education: Computer Criticism vs. Technocentric Thinking." *Educational Researcher,* 16:1 (1987).

Pea, Roy D. "Cognitive Technologies for Mathematics Education." In Alan H. Schoenfeld (Ed.). *Cognitive Science and Mathematics Education.* Hillsdale, N.J.: Lawrence Erlbaum Associates, 1987a, 89-122.

Pea, Roy D. "The Aims of Software Criticism: Reply to Professor Papert." *Educational Researcher,* 16:5 (1987b), 4-8.

Peterson, P.L. "Teaching for Higher-order Thinking in Mathematics: The Challenge for the Next Decade." In Douglas A. Grouws, Thomas J. Cooney, and Douglas Jones (Eds.). *Perspectives on Research on Effective Mathematics Teaching, Volume 1.* Reston, Va.: National Council of Teachers of Mathematics, 1988, 2-26.

Peterson, P.L., and Carpenter, T.L. (Eds.). "Learning Through Instruction: The Study of Students' Thinking During Instruction in Mathematics." A Special Issue of the *Educational Psychologist,* 1989.

Piaget, J. *Ou va L'education?* International Commission on the Development of Education, UNESCO (1948). English Translation. New York: Grossman, 1973.

Piaget, J. *The Construction of Reality in the Child.* New York: Basic Books, 1954.

Polya, G. *How to Solve It.* Princeton, N.J.: Princeton University Press, 1945.

Resnick, Lauren B. "Task Analysis in Instructional Design: Some Cases from Mathematics." In D. Klahr (Ed.). *Cognition and Instruction: Issues and Agendas.* Hillsdale, N.J.: Lawrence Erlbaum Associates, 1976, 51-80.

Resnick, Lauren B. "Mathematics and Science Learning: A New Conception." *Science,* 220 (April 29, 1983), 477-478.

Resnick, Lauren B. *Education and Learning to Think.* Committee on Mathematics, Science, and Technology Education, Commission on Behavioral and Social Sciences and Education, National Research Council. Washington, D.C.: National Academy Press, 1987.

Resnick, Lauren B. "Treating Mathematics as an Ill-Structured Discipline." In Randall I. Charles and Edward A. Silver (Eds.). *The Teaching and Assessing of Mathematical Problem Solving.* Reston, Va.: National Council of Teachers of Mathematics, 1988, 32-60.

Reusser, Kurt. "Problem-Solving Beyond the Logic of Things: Textual and Contextual Effects on Understanding and Solving Word Problems." Paper presented at the annual meeting of the American Educational Research Association, San Francisco, Calif., April 1986.

Rheinboldt, Werner C. *Future Directions in Computational Mathematics, Algorithms, and Scientific Software.* Philadelphia, Pa.: Society for Industrial and Applied Mathematics, 1985.

Rhoads, C. "Organization of Microcomputer Instruction in Secondary Mathematics Education." Dissertation, University of Maryland, 1986.

Romberg, Thomas A. "Policy Implications of the Three R's of Mathematics Education: Revolution, Reform, and Research." Paper presented at the annual meeting of the American Educational Research Association, New Orleans, La., April 1988.

Romberg, Thomas A., and Carpenter, Thomas P. "Research on Teaching and Learning Mathematics: Two Disciplines of Scientific Inquiry." In M.C. Wittrock (Ed.). *Handbook of Research on Teaching, Third Edition.* New York: Macmillan, 1986, 850-873.

Schoen, Harold L. (Ed.). *Estimation and Mental Computation.* 1986 NCTM Yearbook. Reston, Va.: National Council of Teachers of Mathematics, 1986.

Schoenfeld, Alan H. *Mathematical Problem Solving.* New York: Academic Press, 1985.

Schoenfeld, Alan H. (Ed.). *Cognitive Science and Mathematics Education.* Hillsdale, N.J.: Lawrence Erlbaum Associates, 1987.

Schoenfeld, Alan H. "Mathematics, Technology, and Higher-order Thinking." In R. Nickerson (Ed.). *Technology in Education in 2020: Thinking About the Non-too-distant Future.* Hillsdale, N.J.: Lawrence Erlbaum Associates, 1988a.

Schoenfeld, Alan H. "Problem Solving in Context(s)." In Randall I. Charles and Edward A. Silver (Eds.). *The Teaching and Assessing of Mathematical Problem Solving.* Reston, Va.: National Council of Teachers of Mathematics, 1988b.

Schwartz, Judah L., and Yerushalmy, Michal. "Using Microcomputers to Restore Invention to the Learning of Mathematics." In Izaak Wirszup and Robert Streit (Eds.). *Developments in School Mathematics Around the World.* Reston, Va.: National Council of Teachers of Mathematics, 1987, 623-636.

Shavelson, Richard J.; Webb, Noreen M.; Stasz, Cathleen; and McArthur, David. "Teaching Mathematical Problem Solving: Insights from Teachers and Tutors." In Randall I. Charles and Edward A. Silver (Eds.). *The Teaching and Assessing of Mathematical Problem Solving.* Reston, Va.: National Council of Teachers of Mathematics, 1988, 203-231.

Silver, Edward A. *Teaching and Learning Mathematical Problem Solving: Multiple Research Perspectives.* Hillsdale, N.J.: Lawrence Erlbaum Associates, 1985.

Smith, David A.; Porter, Gerald J.; Leinbach, L. Carl; and Wenger, Ronald H. (Eds.). *Computers and Mathematics: The Use of Computers in Undergraduate Instruction.* MAA Notes No. 9. Washington, D.C.: Mathematical Association of America, 1988.

Steen, Lynn Arthur. "The Science of Patterns." *Science,* 240 (April 29, 1988), 611-616.

Steffe, L.P.; von Glasersfeld, E.; Richards, J.; and Cobb, P. *Children's Counting Types: Philosophy, Theory, and Application.* New York: Praeger, 1983.

Stevenson, Harold W.; Lee, S-Y; and Stigler, J.W. "Mathematics Achievement of Chinese, Japanese, and American Children." *Science*, 231 (February 14, 1986), 693-699.

Stigler, James W., and Perry, Michelle. "Cross-Cultural Studies of Mathematics Teaching and Learning: Recent Findings and New Directions." In Douglas A. Grouws, Thomas Cooney, and Douglas Jones (Eds.). *Perspectives on Research on Effective Mathematics Teaching*. Reston, Va.: National Council of Teachers of Mathematics, 1988, 194-223.

Suydam, Marilyn. "An Overview of Research: Computers in Mathematics Education, K-12." *Mathematics Education Digest, No. 1*. ERIC Clearinghouse for Science, Mathematics, and Environmental Education. Columbus: Ohio State University, 1986.

Swift, Jim. "Exploring Data with a Microcomputer." In Viggo P. Hansen (Ed.). *Computers in Mathematics Education*. Reston, Va.: National Council of Teachers of Mathematics, 1984, 107-117.

Walker, Decker F. "LOGO Needs Research: A Response to Papert's Paper." *Educational Researcher*, 16:5 (1987), 9-11.

Wearne, Diana, and Hiebert, James. "A Cognitive Approach to Meaningful Mathematics Instruction: Testing a Local Theory Using Decimal Numbers." *Journal for Research in Mathematics Education*, 19 (November 1988), 371-384.

Wilf, Herbert S. "The Disk with the College Education." *American Mathematical Monthly*, 89 (1982), 4-8.

Yerushalmy, Michal; Chazan, Daniel; and Gordon, Myles. *Guided Inquiry and Technology: A Year Long Study of Children and Teachers Using the Geometric Supposers*. Technical Report TR88-6., Cambridge, Mass.: Educational Technology Center, 1987.

Zorn, Paul. "Computing in Undergraduate Mathematics." *Notices of the American Mathematical Society*, 34 (October 1987), 917-923.

CREDITS FOR RESHAPING SCHOOL MATHEMATICS

MATHEMATICAL SCIENCES EDUCATION BOARD

Editorial Rewrite, Lynn Arthur Steen
Staff Direction, Linda P. Rosen

NATIONAL ACADEMY PRESS

Graphic Design, Susan England
Copy Editor, Barbara Rice
Editorial Coordination, Sally Stanfield

PHOTOGRAPHS COURTESY OF

Fairfax County Public Schools, Virginia (pp. 1, 4, 7, 17, 27, 35, 36, 37, 47)
Montgomery County Public Schools, Maryland (pp. 9, 15, 24)
National Aeronautics and Space Administration (p. 22)

ARTWORK COURTESY OF

The Education Development Center and
    Sunburst Communications
        The Geometric Supposer (p. 13)
National Council of Teachers of Mathematics, adapted
    from *Curriculum and Evaluation Standards for
    School Mathematics*
        Thinking Visually (p. 29)
        Mystery Graph (p. 45)

FINANCIAL SUPPORT

We also wish to thank The Educational Foundation of America, Exxon Education Foundation, National Research Council, National Science Foundation (Directorates for Biological and Behavioral and Social Sciences; Computer and Information Science and Engineering; Engineering; Geosciences; Mathematical and Physical Sciences; and Science and Engineering Education), and The Teagle Foundation for support of the development, publication, and dissemination of this document.